Practical App Development with Aurelia

Leverage the Power of Aurelia to Build Personal and Business Applications

Matthew Duffield

Apress®

Practical App Development with Aurelia

Matthew Duffield
West Linn, Oregon, USA

ISBN-13 (pbk): 978-1-4842-3401-3
https://doi.org/10.1007/978-1-4842-3402-0

ISBN-13 (electronic): 978-1-4842-3402-0

Library of Congress Control Number: 2018936370

Managing Director, Apress Media LLC: Welmoed Spahr
Acquisitions Editor: Louise Corrigan
Development Editor: James Markham
Coordinating Editor: Nancy Chen

Cover designed by eStudioCalamar

Cover image by Freepik (www.freepik.com)

Distributed to the book trade worldwide by Springer Science+Business Media New York, 233 Spring Street, 6th Floor, New York, NY 10013. Phone 1-800-SPRINGER, fax (201) 348-4505, e-mail orders-ny@springer-sbm.com, or visit www.springeronline.com. Apress Media, LLC is a California LLC and the sole member (owner) is Springer Science + Business Media Finance Inc (SSBM Finance Inc). SSBM Finance Inc is a **Delaware** corporation.

For information on translations, please e-mail rights@apress.com, or visit http://www.apress.com/rights-permissions.

Apress titles may be purchased in bulk for academic, corporate, or promotional use. eBook versions and licenses are also available for most titles. For more information, reference our Print and eBook Bulk Sales web page at http://www.apress.com/bulk-sales.

Any source code or other supplementary material referenced by the author in this book is available to readers on GitHub via the book's product page, located at www.apress.com/9781484234013. For more detailed information, please visit http://www.apress.com/source-code.

Printed on acid-free paper

For my wife Erica and my kids Dean, Duncan, and Veronica,
who have patiently endured letting me finish a sentence or
a coding sample before asking a question or inviting me to play.
I love you all very much.

Table of Contents

About the Author xiii

About the Technical Reviewer xv

Acknowledgments xvii

Chapter 1: Introduction... 1

What Is Aurelia? 1

What Is MVVM? 2

When Do I Need a Front-End Framework?... 2

Why Should I Use Aurelia? 3

Setting Expectations 4

Summary... 5

Chapter 2: Getting Set Up 7

Build Options... 7

Configuring your machine.. 8

ES6 and TypeScript 9

NodeJS.. 9

Aurelia CLI 10

Hello World 21

Summary... 22

Chapter 3: Routing.. 23

Router Configuration 23

Push State Configuration 29

Dynamic Routes 30

Child Routers... 33

View Ports 35

Layouts 37

Redirecting Routes 40

Unknown Routes 40

Fallback Route 41

Summary 42

Chapter 4: Security and Pipelines 43

Router Pipelines 43

Authorize Step 44

Audit Step 47

Summary 49

Chapter 5: Dependency Injection 51

Dependency Injection in Aurelia 51

Manual Injection 52

Injection by Decorator 54

Autoinjection 55

Dependency Injection Containers 56

Container Management 57

Dependency Injection Resolvers 58

Summary 59

Chapter 6: Services 61

Summary 66

Chapter 7: Getting Data 67

HTTP Client 67

HTTP Fetch Client 74

Limitations to Fetch 76

Interceptors 76

Summary 79

Chapter 8: Data Binding...**81**

Data Binding and Event Binding...81

Binding...81

   Types of Binding 81

   Referencing Elements in Bindings...82

   Input 83

   Check Box..83

   Radio 86

   Select 87

   Element Content 90

   Class/Style..91

   Conditionals..93

   Binding Scopes..95

   Looping...96

   Value Converters 97

   Binding Behaviors..97

DOM Events..98

   Types of Binding 98

   Delegate 98

   Trigger 99

   Call...99

Summary..100

Chapter 9: Templates **101**

Templates..101

   String Interpolation..101

   Conditional Expressions 102

   View Resource Pipeline 103

   Slots 104

   Composition...105

   "as-element" Attribute 105

Summary..106

Chapter 10: Forms and Validation 107

HTML Form Element.. 107

Aurelia Validation Plug-in 109

Summary.. 116

Chapter 11: View and Component Life Cycles 117

View Life Cycles... 117

Component Life Cycles 118

Summary.. 119

Chapter 12: Event Aggregation 121

Setting Up Our Shell.. 121

Manage Your Subscriptions 125

Alternative Approach.. 126

Summary.. 126

Chapter 13: Custom Elements 127

What Are Custom Elements?... 127

Static Custom Elements 127

Standard Custom Elements... 129

Advanced Custom Elements 139

Summary.. 146

Chapter 14: Custom Attributes 147

Defining Custom Attributes 147

Set-Focus Custom Attribute 147

Input-Mask Custom Attribute 150

Circle Custom Attribute 156

Summary.. 159

Chapter 15: Value Converters 161

Value Converters.. 161

Conventions 161

Building Your First Value Converter 162

    Multiple Parameters 164

    Parameters as Objects 168

    Making Your Value Converters Global 169

Summary 170

Chapter 16: Binding Behaviors 171

Binding Behaviors 171

Custom Binding Behaviors 174

Summary 177

Chapter 17: Compose 179

When Not to Use Compose 179

When to Use Compose 179

Summary 183

Chapter 18: Dynamic Views 185

getViewStrategy 185

Enhance 189

Summary 194

Chapter 19: Creating Features 195

What Are Features? 195

Configuring Global Resources 196

Markup Scenario 198

Summary 199

Chapter 20: Creating Plug-ins 201

Going from a Feature to a Plug-in 201

Existing Aurelia CLI Project 202

Publishing your Plug-in 208

Using Your Plug-in 209

Summary 210

Chapter 21: Animations **211**

Animation Plug-ins... 211

Aurelia-Animator-CSS Plug-in... 211

    CSS3 Animations 212

    Animations and Routes.. 212

    Getting Our Animations Set Up 213

    Adding/Removing Items 217

Summary.. 223

Chapter 22: Dialogs **225**

Aurelia Dialog Plug-in 225

Global Dialog Settings.. 231

Styling Dialogs 231

Summary.. 232

Chapter 23: Localization **233**

Aurelia i18n Plug-in 233

    Translations with nested objects... 239

Summary.. 240

Chapter 24: Testing and Debugging **241**

Unit Testing 241

    Testing Custom Elements 242

    Mocking Dependencies 245

End-to-End Testing... 247

    Interacting with the Browser 248

Debugging Aurelia Applications 249

    View-Spy 249

    Compile-Spy 251

    Aurelia Inspector in Chrome 252

Summary.. 254

Chapter 25: Bundling and Deploying **255**

Bundling 255

Deploying 262

Deployment Best Practices 264

Summary 264

Chapter 26: Closing Thoughts **265**

Index **267**

....

About the Author

Matthew Duffield is an author, consultant, and trainer and has more than 18 years of development experience. He has his own consulting business called Summit Software. He has received various Microsoft MVP awards and always tries to further his knowledge by learning other frameworks and languages. The bulk of his experience is in .NET, JavaScript, NodeJS, and architecting data warehouse solutions along with business intelligence. He is the creator of FrontEnd Creator, an online editor for building Aurelia applications without any server-side setup. You can find it at `www.frontendcreator.com`. You can also follow him on Twitter at @mattduffield or visit his blog on WordPress.

About the Technical Reviewer

Gary Gambill has been working with Information Systems since the late 90s. He has a diverse background that encompasses a broad swath of an organization's information life cycle. This includes areas such as Software Development, Business Intelligence Architecture, Network and Storage System Design, and Data/Information Architecture. Combined, these areas of technical leadership help him to understand and rapidly accelerate almost any organization's Digital Enterprise transformation.

Acknowledgments

Thanks go out to my parents for getting our first computer, a TI-99, and letting me spend countless hours writing code from the monthly code magazines and then complain for the rest of the month when there was an error.

Thanks to my loving wife and kids for putting up with my late hours and closed-door policy. You guys were great and I appreciate all of your support.

Finally, thanks to Rob Eisenberg and the whole Aurelia team for creating such a wonderful framework. Building applications has never been more exciting and fun!

CHAPTER 1

Introduction

Technology is constantly changing, and this makes it difficult to keep up on everything new. Web technology is no different, and it seems that there is a new library or framework showing up every couple of months. In this chapter we'll take a quick look at some of these technological developments and what to expect in the rest of the book.

What Is Aurelia?

Aurelia is a relatively new kid on the block when it comes to frameworks. It was first introduced back in 2015 by Rob Eisenberg. It is a framework that is meant to cover the spectrum of web, mobile, and desktop development. It is a framework that utilizes convention over configuration. This is nice in that if you follow the simple conventions you gain a lot of efficiencies. It is also a framework that is unobtrusive, meaning that it does its job extremely well while staying out of your way. You will find, as you develop an application using Aurelia, that you are not fighting the framework to get your work accomplished. This is itself a big point for convincing anyone to using Aurelia. Finally, Aurelia is standards-based. This means that it tries to remain pure to adhering to ECMAScript specifications. Writing web applications using JavaScript can be frustrating, but with ECMAScript 2015 and ECMAScript 2016, we have a lot of advancements to the language specification. Some of the features you can use natively now, but others require a transpiler like Babel. You will see that the majority of code examples are either ECMAScript 2015 or TypeScript.

One important aspect of how Aurelia came to be so rich and mature as a framework is its creator, Rob Eisenberg. For Eisenberg, Aurelia has been a culmination of previous frameworks and patterns he has used with frameworks he has built for other technologies. First we see Caliburn, a XAML framework for building applications targeting Windows Presentation Framework (WPF) and Silverlight. Next, he introduced Caliburn.Micro, which was a revamp of the previous framework but smaller and simpler.

1

© Matthew Duffield 2018
M. Duffield, *Practical App Development with Aurelia*, https://doi.org/10.1007/978-1-4842-3402-0_1

He then decided to target the Web with his next framework, Durandal. It is still in use, and it was very much a precursor to what we were going to get with Aurelia. Finally, Aurelia was announced and the rest is history.

Whether it is two-way data binding or routing, Aurelia is a framework that really shines. Because it is standards-based, you find that a lot of what you are being introduced to is not some proprietary format; rather, it is the same as what you would use in JavaScript.

What Is MVVM?

Most modern frameworks try to solve the issue of binding elements on web pages to some backing controller JavaScript file. Libraries such as Backbone, jQuery, or Knockout tried to help alleviate the amount of work required to get data to and from HTML elements. The term model-view-view-model (MVVM) really came out of the introduction to XAML technology within Microsoft. It was an attempt to create a data context that your page was aware of and could bind to. This same principle applies to Aurelia and most modern front-end frameworks. Your web page has some form of binding context in which it can create binding on HTML elements and then receive updates from the view model.

With MVVM in Aurelia, you have a rich data-binding paradigm. Aurelia takes this even one step further with its conventions. If, for example, you are creating bindings inside an HTML Form element, Aurelia will automatically create those bindings as two-way. This means that you can send changes from the page to the view model as well as update the page from the view model.

If we couple Aurelia with ECMAScript 2015 and string interpolation, we find that we already understand how Aurelia works when it comes to displaying data-bound information.

When Do I Need a Front-End Framework?

You may be a seasoned web developer veteran and can recall the days when you wrote all of your web pages using pure HTML, JavaScript, and CSS. You still can do this, but as your web pages transitioned to fully functional applications, you started seeing the need for a framework to help you with all the architectural concerns when building a web application.

A front-end framework is going to help you with solving the complex patterns of building a modern single-page application. It should handle the following:

- Data binding

- Routing

- Communication across screens

- Support separation of concerns

- Dependency injection/inversion of control

Not all front-end frameworks will handle every one of these bullet points, but the majority of mature ones will. A good rule of thumb for a framework that does its job well is that it can accomplish all of these bullet points while being completely unobtrusive, not forcing you into learning a slew of proprietary concepts.

Why Should I Use Aurelia?

So why should you use Aurelia? What about it makes it compelling and attractive? Aurelia is here to stay and has a very large self-supporting community. There is a Gitter channel for Aurelia where you can ask for help as you develop your applications. Recently a Discourse site was setup for more community interaction. Aurelia has a host of developers that maintain and support its core components. However, since it is open sourced, you have the ability to provide pull requests and make it even better as you start developing your own applications.

Aurelia is extremely easy to learn. There many examples providing capabilities and features including the Skeleton Navigation samples. You can pick the example using JavaScript or TypeScript and the bundler of your choice. You also have the ability to use the Aurelia CLI to quickly get your application up and running from scratch. The Aurelia CLI, or command-line interface, allows developers to quickly scaffold and setup a new Aurelia project with little effort. It provides a wide range of options to choose from or you can just use the default settings.

Aurelia is a framework which uses patterns that are simple yet comprehensive. It is surprising how easy it is to develop applications, even extremely complex ones, using Aurelia.

If you are getting ready to start a new project, or if you are just plain curious, getting started with Aurelia is a breeze.

Setting Expectations

Over the remainder of this book, we will be covering different aspects of developing web applications using Aurelia. Here is a quick synopsis of what each chapter will entail.

Chapter 2 is all about getting your development machine set up for creating your first Aurelia application. It will cover options for where you can start, and it will present the language choices of JavaScript (ECMAScript 2015) and TypeScript. It will address dependencies like NodeJS and bundlers like Webpack.

Chapter 3 will cover setting up your first routes and dive deeper into what makes the Aurelia router.

Chapter 4 will piggyback off of routing and handle security and pipelines.

Chapter 5 will take a look at dependency injection.

Chapter 6 will cover creating services that will be used across multiple screens.

Chapter 7 will look at getting our data using both HTTP Client and Fetch Client. It will also look at interceptors and how we can use them in our application.

In Chapter 8, we will take a look at Aurelia rich data binding, including one-way and two-way events and looping.

In Chapter 9, we cover building your views using templates including string interpolation and requiring dependencies in HTML.

Chapter 10 will go a step further and look at HTML Form and validation.

Chapter 11 will present you with an understanding of Aurelia view and component life cycles.

Chapter 12 will introduce you to the Event Aggregator and how you can use it to communicate across your view model and services.

Chapter 13 will show you how to create custom elements.

Chapter 14 will show you how to create custom attributes.

Chapter 15 will show you how to create value converters.

Chapter 16 will show you how to create binding behaviors.

Chapter 17 will introduce the compose custom element and how it can be used in dynamic scenarios.

Chapter 18 will introduce creating dynamic views.

Chapter 19 will introduce how to take our custom elements and custom attributes and wrap them up in an Aurelia feature.

Chapter 20 will introduce how you can further encapsulate your feature and change it to a stand-alone Aurelia plug-in.

Chapter 21 will introduce using animations when navigating routes as well as adding and removing items.

Chapter 22 will introduce using dialogs in your application.

Chapter 23 will introduce using localization in your application.

Chapter 24 will walk you through testing and debugging your application.

Chapter 25 will cover bundling and deploying your application.

Chapter 26 will summarize all that we have learned with key reminders of important concepts.

Summary

Learning a new front-end framework can be daunting. To stay relevant and competitive, we need to constantly be evaluating and learning new tools. Aurelia is one of the tools that is a must-have for your collective toolbox. Throughout the rest of this book, we will focus on building your arsenal with the knowledge and understanding to go out and build modern single-page applications using Aurelia.

CHAPTER 2

Getting Set Up

Getting started in Aurelia gives you a lot of freedom. There are a lot of different approaches you can take to setting up your environment just the way you like. This is one of the biggest attractions to Aurelia: it is very unobtrusive.

Build Options

Let's take a look at several different options you have with regard to getting your environment set up using Aurelia:

- Aurelia CLI

- Webpack

- JSPM

Each of these options provides you with building and bundling your application. Aurelia CLI is by far the newest one and is constantly being updated with new features. Webpack is probably the most popular on the market. JSPM is still viable but no longer the new shiny build tool the other two represent.

For the remainder of this book, we will be focusing on the Aurelia CLI, but everything that we will cover that is specific to the Aurelia CLI is possible with either Webpack or JSPM.

© Matthew Duffield 2018
M. Duffield, *Practical App Development with Aurelia*, https://doi.org/10.1007/978-1-4842-3402-0_2

Configuring your machine

There are a few dependencies that you will need to have installed in order to use Aurelia effectively. The following is a list of dependencies:

- Node.js – install NodeJS version 4.x or above

- Git – install your favorite Git client

After you have these dependencies installed, we will move on with using the Node Package Manager (NPM) to install the Aurelia CLI. From a command line, execute the following command:

```
npm install -g aurelia-cli
```

This command will install the Aurelia CLI globally.

Note   If your OS is Mac or Linux, it is recommended to always run your command from a Bash prompt. You may also need to use sudo when you execute global commands.

If everything was successful, then you should have an output similar to Figure 2-1.

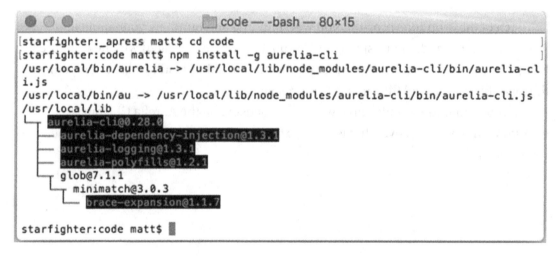

Figure 2-1. *Installing aurelia-cli*

ES6 and TypeScript

Aurelia is one of the available frameworks that are future facing. What this means is that it was written targeting the latest features of the ECMAScript specification. This allows us to use features that are part of the ECMAScript 2015 and ECMAScript 2016 specification. Most developers will either choose to develop their applications using ECMA-2015 version of JavaScript or use TypeScript. TypeScript is a transpiler that provides typing plus a ton of other great features for developing large JavaScript applications. If you are familiar with C# or Java, you will find using TypeScript very easy to use.

We will be using ECMAScript 2015 as our basis for developing our applications. We still get a lot of cool features that will make creating your Aurelia application very fun. As not all browsers support all of the features currently, we will be using Babel as our transpiler to generate ECMAScript 5.

Note   Beginning in Chapter 3, we will be using Chrome as our browser.

NodeJS

Although NodeJS is used heavily with all of the build systems available for Aurelia, you do not need to be an expert on NodeJS. There are only a handful of useful commands that you must be aware of:

- npm install --save aurelia-dialog

This statement installs the Aurelia Dialog plug-in and saves it in the package.json. You will notice a little later that the Aurelia CLI also provides a similar feature that not only installs the plug-in but also configures it so that it is bundled correctly.

- npm install --save `https://github.com/<account>/<project>`

The preceding statement provides you the ability to install packages that reside on GitHub but have not yet been published to NPM. You will find that not all of the packages that you want have been published to NPM, and this will still give you the flexibility to use both.

> **Note**   If you are new to using NodeJS or NPM, it might be helpful to familiarize yourself so that you understand the syntax and how it works.

Aurelia CLI

Alright, let's turn our attention to the Aurelia CLI and walk through all the steps required with setting up your first application. Open up a terminal window or command prompt and execute the following code:

```
au new
```

You should see something similar to the output in Figure 2-2.

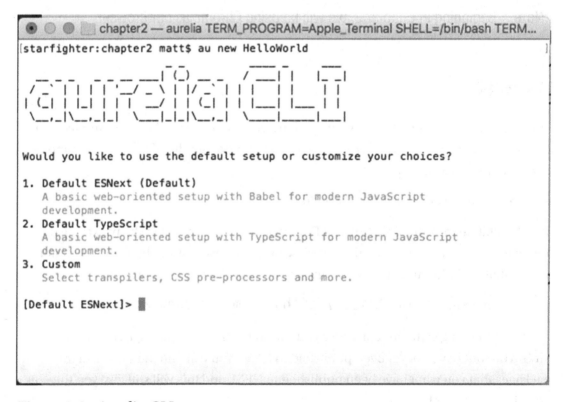

Figure 2-2. *Aurelia-CLI*

As you can see, the Aurelia CLI really tries to help you even if you have never used it before. Let's go ahead and try creating our first project. We will call it "HelloWorld". Execute the following statement in your terminal:

```
au new helloworld
```

You should see the output shown in Figure 2-3.

Figure 2-3. *Aurelia-CLI new project*

We are presented with three different options. We could simply hit enter and select the default setting as it is what we will be using in the book. Select number 3 and you'll be presented with two more default transpilers (Babel or TypeScript) as shown in Figure 2-4.

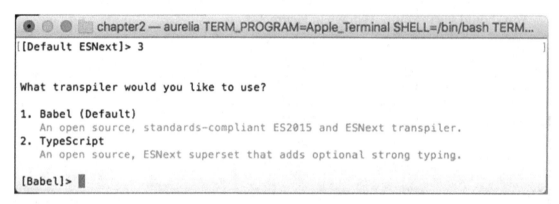

Figure 2-4. *Aurelia-CLI selecting transpiler*

Select Babel (1) and we are asked about how we would like our templates set up. Here, we have three options as to the level of minification we want the bundler to do (Figure 2-5). When we deploy an application, we are going to want to have the smallest footprint. We will go ahead and select option 3 for maximum minification.

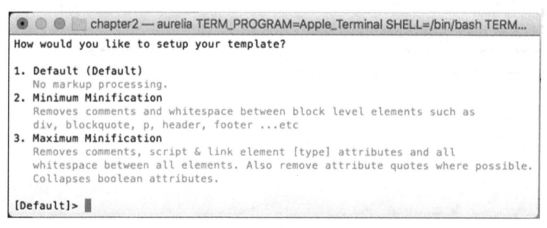

Figure 2-5. *Aurelia CLI template minification*

Again, we are given options as to what type of CSS development we wish to use. We will be using pure CSS, so let's go ahead and select option 1 (Figure 2-6).

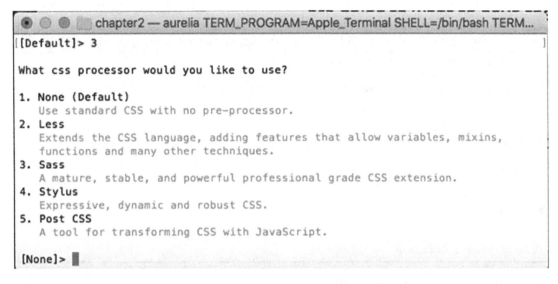

Figure 2-6. *Aurelia CLI CSS processor*

We are now presented with the option to have our project configured to handle unit tests. Let's go ahead and select option 1 (Figure 2-7).

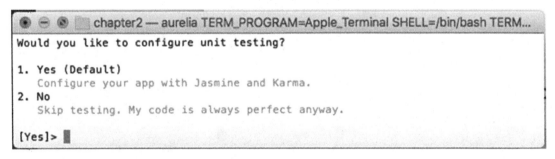

Figure 2-7. *Aurelia CLI unit testing*

Next, we are presented with a selection of editors that we are going to use. Visual Studio Code has quickly become a very popular editor in its short lifespan. Although you can use any of the options in Figure 2-8, select default editor (option 1).

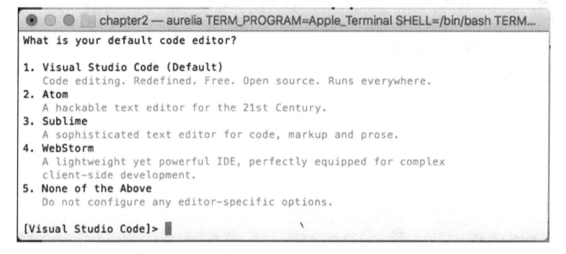

Figure 2-8. *Aurelia CLI code editor*

We are finally getting close to finishing the project. A project review screen shows all of our selections (Figure 2-9). Here, you can continue and create the project, restart the wizard, or completely abort. Let's keep moving forward to select Yes (Option 1).

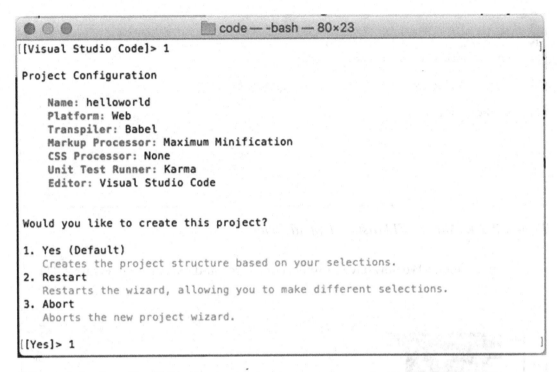

```
● ● ●                    📁 code — -bash — 80×23
[[Visual Studio Code]> 1

Project Configuration

    Name: helloworld
    Platform: Web
    Transpiler: Babel
    Markup Processor: Maximum Minification
    CSS Processor: None
    Unit Test Runner: Karma
    Editor: Visual Studio Code


Would you like to create this project?

1. Yes (Default)
   Creates the project structure based on your selections.
2. Restart
   Restarts the wizard, allowing you to make different selections.
3. Abort
   Aborts the new project wizard.

[[Yes]> 1
```

Figure 2-9. *Aurelia CLI project review*

We are now presented with our final question. We can choose either to have the CLI install all of our dependencies or to decide not to do it now. You can still install the dependencies by executing the following command if you so desire:

```
npm install
```

We are going to let the CLI handle the installation for us and select the default option 1 (Figure 2-10).

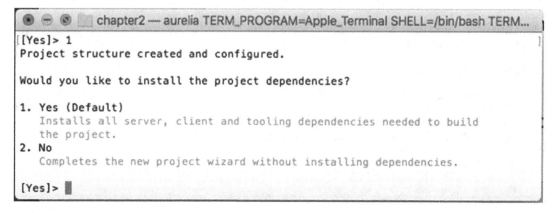

Figure 2-10. *Aurelia CLI install dependencies*

Congratulations! We now have a project configured and ready to use (Figure 2-11).

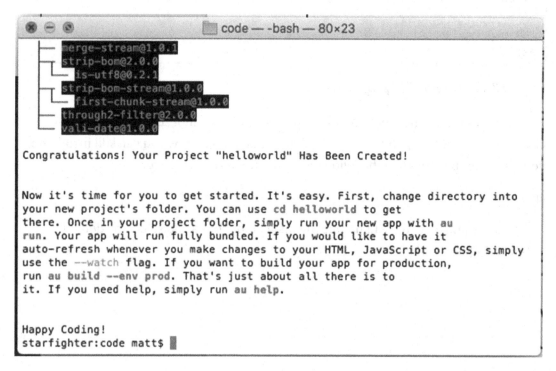

Figure 2-11. *Aurelia CLI install complete*

We are given a few tips that are worth noting for future reference, namely, the commands that we can do to run and build our application. Let's list them out next:

- au run
- au run --watch
- au build
- au build --env prod
- au help

With these commands, we will be able to handle running our application as well as bundling it. As the documentation states, it is possible use a watch flag so that any changes saved in your editor will automatically relaunch your browser so that you don't have to build with every code change.

Now that we have the project set up, let's see what kind of help we get from the CLI:

```
cd helloworld
au help
```

Figure 2-12 shows the output that the CLI will generate for us.

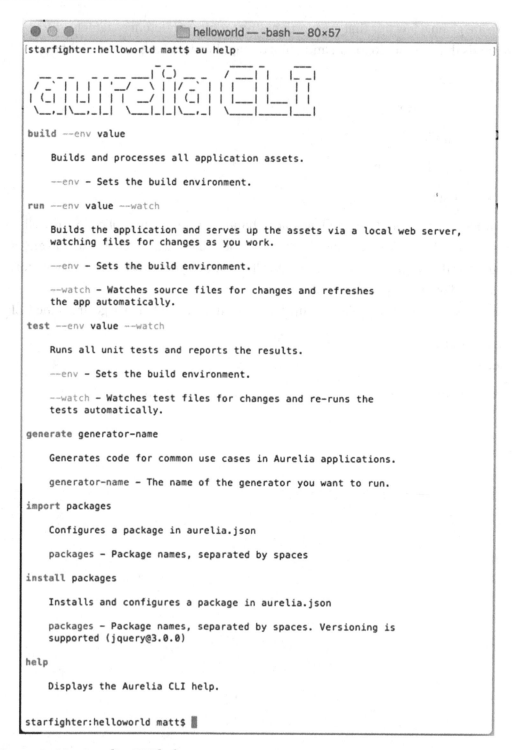

```
[starfighter:helloworld matt$ au help

  __ _ _   _ _ __ ___| (_) __ _     ___| |   |_ _|
 / _` | | | | '__/ _ \ | |/ _` |   / __| |    | |
| (_| | |_| | | |  __/ | | (_| |  | (__| |___ | |
 \__,_|\__,_|_|  \___|_|_|\__,_|   \___|_____|___|


build --env value

    Builds and processes all application assets.

    --env - Sets the build environment.

run --env value --watch

    Builds the application and serves up the assets via a local web server,
    watching files for changes as you work.

    --env - Sets the build environment.

    --watch - Watches source files for changes and refreshes
    the app automatically.

test --env value --watch

    Runs all unit tests and reports the results.

    --env - Sets the build environment.

    --watch - Watches test files for changes and re-runs the
    tests automatically.

generate generator-name

    Generates code for common use cases in Aurelia applications.

    generator-name - The name of the generator you want to run.

import packages

    Configures a package in aurelia.json

    packages - Package names, separated by spaces

install packages

    Installs and configures a package in aurelia.json

    packages - Package names, separated by spaces. Versioning is
    supported (jquery@3.0.0)

help

    Displays the Aurelia CLI help.


starfighter:helloworld matt$
```

Figure 2-12. *Aurelia CLI help*

The following describes the options listed in Figure 2-12:

- build – allows us to build application as well target a specific environment

- run – allows us to run our application targeting a specific environment as well as setting the watch flag for automatic updates to the browser

- test – provides testing your application as well as targeting a specific environment. You can also use the watch flag for your tests

- generate – provides the ability to generate common use cases, as shown in Figure 2-13

- import – provides the ability to configure packages in the aurelia.json file. These packages have already been installed typically by using: 'npm install ...'

- install – provides the ability to install and configure a package in the aurelia.json file

- help – provides help documentation

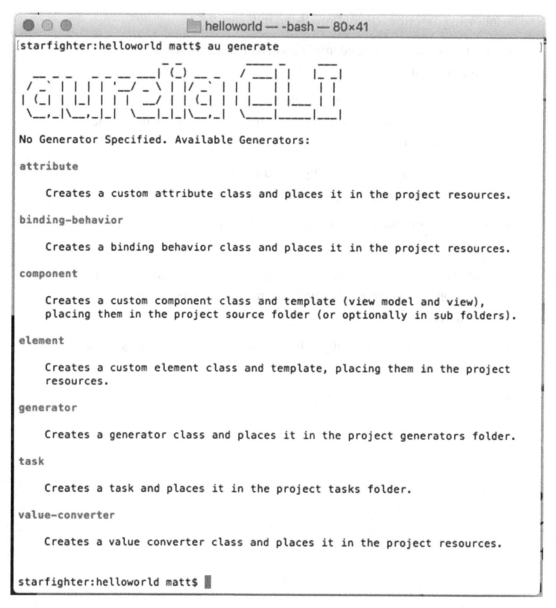

Figure 2-13. *Aurelia CLI generate*

As you can see from the preceding image, you have several options. If you have used scaffolding tools, such as Yeoman, then this should be very familiar. One nice thing about this generator is that you can extend it and create your generator as well.

Hello World

We have exhausted what we can do the Aurelia CLI. Let's wrap up by running the application. Execute the following statement in your bash terminal:

`au run`

You should see something like the output in Figure 2-14.

```
● ● ●     helloworld — aurelia TERM_PROGRAM=Apple_Terminal SHELL=/bin/bash — 80...
[starfighter:helloworld matt$ au run
Starting 'readProjectConfiguration'...
Finished 'readProjectConfiguration'
Starting 'processMarkup'...
Starting 'processCSS'...
Starting 'copyFiles'...
Starting 'configureEnvironment'...
Finished 'copyFiles'
Finished 'processCSS'
Finished 'processMarkup'
Finished 'configureEnvironment'
Starting 'buildJavaScript'...
Finished 'buildJavaScript'
Starting 'writeBundles'...
Tracing app...
Tracing environment...
Tracing main...
Tracing resources/index...
Tracing app...
Tracing aurelia-binding...
Tracing aurelia-bootstrapper...
Tracing aurelia-dependency-injection...
Tracing aurelia-event-aggregator...
Tracing aurelia-framework...
Tracing aurelia-history...
Tracing aurelia-history-browser...
Tracing aurelia-loader-default...
Tracing aurelia-logging-console...
Tracing aurelia-pal-browser...
Tracing aurelia-route-recognizer...
Tracing aurelia-router...
Tracing aurelia-templating-binding...
Tracing text...
Tracing aurelia-templating-resources...
Tracing aurelia-templating-router...
Tracing aurelia-testing...
Writing app-bundle.js...
Writing vendor-bundle.js...
Finished 'writeBundles'
Application Available At: http://localhost:9001
BrowserSync Available At: http://localhost:3002
```

Figure 2-14. *Aurelia CLI run*

Now, in a browser of your choice if you navigate to the URL http://localhost:9001, you should see the result in Figure 2-15.

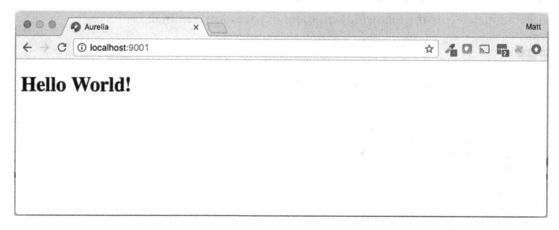

Figure 2-15. *Aurelia CLI browser*

Summary

We have covered a lot of ground here. We now have a fairly good understanding of the Aurelia CLI and the requirements for getting a project up and running. Remember that there is always help online and with the CLI itself if you get stuck or are not sure of something. There are also a lot of example applications that you can clone from GitHub and use for further understanding.

CHAPTER 3

Routing

Aurelia supports routing out of the box. There is no additional work needed to bring in the router. You simply need to configure your router and use the 'router-view' custom element. In this chapter, we will be going over the capabilities and power of routing in Aurelia.

Router Configuration

Getting your application configured to use Aurelia's router only takes a few steps. First, you need to ensure that you have a 'router-view' custom element on your view. A typical example of this would be placing this custom element in your app.html file. Consider the following example:

```
<template>
  <require from="./app.css"></require>
  <require from="./nav-bar.html"></require>

  <nav-bar router.bind="*router"></nav-bar>

  <div class="page-host router">
    <router-view></router-view>
  </div>
</template>
```

This example actually has a lot more going on than adding the 'router-view' custom element but it is a more comprehensive example of what you would really have on your app.html file. We first are bringing in some custom styling. Next, we are requiring a custom element, 'nav-bar'. We use this custom element for providing a menu structure for our routes. As you can see from the 'nav-bar' custom element tag, we bind the property 'router' to a public property on the app.js file with the same name. Next, we have a DIV element that simply has some classes that make it act as a host to the 'router-view' custom element. Finally, we have our 'router-view' custom element.

23

© Matthew Duffield 2018
M. Duffield, *Practical App Development with Aurelia*, https://doi.org/10.1007/978-1-4842-3402-0_3

Let's now look at what the app.js file would look like:

```
import 'jQuery';
import 'bootstrap';

export class App {

  configureRouter(config, router) {
    config.title = 'Routing';
    config.map([
      {route: ["", "page1"], moduleId: "src/page1", href: "#/page1",
      title: "Page 1", nav: true},
      {route: "page2", moduleId: "src/page2", href: "#/page2", title:
      "Page 2", nav: true},
      {route: "page3", moduleId: "src/page3", href: "#/page3", title:
      "Page 3", nav: true},
    ]);

    this.router = router;
  }
}
```

As you can see from this example, we have a single function in our App class called "configureRouter". In this function we can set the title of our HTML document by setting the 'title' property. We can also supply an array of route objects, RouteConfig, that will make up where our router can navigate. We finally set the 'router' object to a class-level member so that we can bind against it like we saw in our app.html file. Notice that we can specify a 'default' route by specifying an empty string ("") as the 'route' property. By specifying a default route, you can handle for an URL address that has no hash value.

Let's take a closer look at everything we can do with the individual RouteConfig objects:

- route – this is the pattern the router uses to match against incoming navigation requests. This can be a single string value or an array of strings. You default a 'default' route by adding an empty string ("")

- moduleId – this is the moduleId of a view model that should be activated

- href – this string represents the URL fragment to navigate. This is required if your route pattern has any dynamic parts to it

- title – this string represents the document title to be set when the route is active

- nav – this Boolean determines if this route will become part of the 'navigation' property. It is this property that is used for creating menus. You can also specify a number and this will set the sort order of the route item

Here is a list of other properties that you can set on a RouteConfig object as well:

- name – this is a unique name for the route. You can use the router to navigate by name of a route instead of by the route pattern

- redirect – this string represents a URL fragment to redirect when this route is matched

- navigationStrategy – this is a function that can be used to dynamically select the module or modules to activate. It receives a current NavigationInstruction and should configure the 'instruction.config' with the appropriate moduleId, viewPorts, or redirect

- viewPorts – this allows you to reference named router-view instances. By supplying a moduleId for each viewPort, the router knows what to activate. It is also possible to provide optional properties related to layout: 'layoutView', 'layoutViewModel', and 'layoutModel'

- settings – this allows you to attach arbitrary data to the route. This is useful when using pipelines and custom data is needed

- caseSensitive – this Boolean determines if the current route is case sensitive or not

- activationStrategy – this string allows you to determine the activation strategy of the route's view model. The available values are 'invoke-lifecycle' and 'replace'

- layoutView – this string represents the file name of the view to be used

- layoutViewModel – this string represents the moduleId of the view model to be used

- layoutModel – this string represents the model parameter to be passed to the view model's 'activate' function

We have our router now configured with three views. Let's take a quick look at the nav-bar.html file to see how we are creating our menu:

```
<template bindable="router">
  <nav class="navbar navbar-default navbar-fixed-top" role="navigation">
    <div class="navbar-header">
      <button type="button" class="navbar-toggle" data-toggle="collapse"
      data-target="#navbar-collapse">
        <span class="sr-only">Toggle Navigation</span>
        <span class="icon-bar"></span>
        <span class="icon-bar"></span>
        <span class="icon-bar"></span>
      </button>
      <a class="navbar-brand" href="#">
        <i class="fa fa-home"></i>
        <span>${router.title}</span>
      </a>
    </div>

    <div class="collapse navbar-collapse" id="navbar-collapse">
      <ul class="nav navbar-nav">
        <li repeat.for="row of router.navigation" class="${row.isActive ?
        'active' : ''}">
          <a data-toggle="collapse" data-target="#navbar-collapse.in" href.
          bind="row.href">${row.title}</a>
        </li>
      </ul>

      <ul class="nav navbar-nav navbar-right">
        <li class="loader" if.bind="router.isNavigating">
          <i class="fa fa-spinner fa-spin fa-2x"></i>
        </li>
```

```
    </ul>
   </div>
  </nav>
</template>
```

If you are familiar with Twitter Bootstrap, then this example should not look foreign. The majority of the markup is necessary for making the menu responsive. Looking at the TEMPLATE tag, we see that we are identifying a property 'router' to be bindable for consumers of this custom element. Next, you will see that we see the following, '${router. title}'. This simply takes the title from the router object and renders in the SPAN element.

If we continue, we will see the next item we encounter is the LI element, which uses a 'repeat.for' syntax. This is where we reference the 'navigation' property off of the router. If you recall, we add our routes to this object by setting the 'nav' property to true or provide a sort order number. We also see that we are updating the class of the LI element to the value of 'active' whenever the route is active; otherwise the value is simply an empty string. Next, we have an A tag that is binding its 'href' property to the 'href' property of the route. We also see that we are displaying the 'title' property of the route inside the A tag.

The final set of markup elements represents a busy indicator. We see that we are binding the 'if' attribute of the LI element in order to create this element when the router is navigating.

With our menu complete, let's take a look at what our application looks like (Figure 3-1).

Figure 3-1. *Page 1 route*

As you can see from the preceding screenshot, we have a nice menu with a title as well as the title for each of the routes. Here is the CSS markup that was used to style our application:

```css
.page-host {
  position: absolute;
  left: 0;
  right: 0;
  top: 50px;
  bottom: 0;
  overflow-x: hidden;
  overflow-y: auto;
}
.router section {
  padding: 20px;
  position: absolute;
  width: 100%;
  height: 100%;
}
.page1 {
  background-color: lightskyblue;
}
.page2 {
  background-color: limegreen;
}
.page3 {
  background-color: lightsalmon;
}
```

There really isn't anything notable about the preceding CSS but it is provided for completeness.

Push State Configuration

Aurelia's router also supports push state instead of relying on hashes. The default behavior is to use hashes, but configuring the router for push state is only a matter of a couple steps. In your index.html file, ensure that you add the following:

```
<!doctype html>
<html>
  <head>
    <title>apress-routing</title>
    <meta charset="utf-8">
    <meta http-equiv="X-UA-Compatible" content="IE=edge">
<meta name="viewport" content="width=device-width, initial-scale=1.0,
maximum-scale=1.0, user-scalable=no"/>
    <link href="https://maxcdn.bootstrapcdn.com/bootstrap/3.3.6/
    css/bootstrap.min.css" rel="stylesheet" integrity="sha384-1q8m
    TJOASx8j1Au+a5WDVnPi2lkFfwwEAa8hDDdjZlpLegxhjVME1fgjWPGmkzs7"
    crossorigin="anonymous">
    <base href="/">
  </head>
  <body aurelia-app="main">
    <h1>Loading...</h1>
    <script src="scripts/vendor-bundle.js" data-main="aurelia-
bootstrapper"></script>
</body>
</html>
```

You can see that we have a BASE tag that set's the 'href' property to the value "/".

Let's now look at what we need to do in order to get our router configured for push state in the app.js file:

```
import 'jQuery';
import 'bootstrap';

export class App {

  configureRouter(config, router) {
    config.title = 'Routing';
    config.options.pushState = true;
```

```
    config.options.root = "/";
    config.map([
      {route: ["", "page1"], moduleId: "src/page1", href: "page1",
      title: "Page 1", nav: true},
      {route: "page2", moduleId: "src/page2", href: "page2", title:
      "Page 2", nav: true},
      {route: "page3", moduleId: "src/page3", href: "page3", title:
      "Page 3", nav: true},
    ]);

    this.router = router;
  }
}
```

You can see that we introduced two new config.options entries. The first simply tells the router it is using push state. The next entry specifies the root. This root value must match what we set up on the index.html file using the BASE tag. Finally, you may have noticed that we removed the hashes from the 'href' entries for each route.

This is all that you have to do to get the front-end portion of your application to support push state. Just remember that push state requires server-side support. You will need to configure your server accordingly depending on how you are supporting your application.

Dynamic Routes

There will be times where you want your routes to be dynamic with regard to the context of the current route. For example, you may have a route that displays a list of orders. It would be nice if you had a link on each order entry that would show the order details. You want your router to support an order-detail route but you need a dynamic order ID. Let's look at the following configuration on how this can be accomplished:

```
import 'jQuery';
import 'bootstrap';

export class App {

  configureRouter(config, router) {
```

```
config.title = 'Routing';
config.map([
  {route: ["", "welcome"], moduleId: "src/welcome", href: "#/welcome",
  title: "Welcome", nav: true},
  {route: "orders", moduleId: "src/orders", href: "#/orders",
  title: "Orders", nav: true},
  {route: "orders/:id", moduleId: "src/order-details", title:
  "Order Details", nav: false},
]);

this.router = router;
  }
}
```

We have three routes defined. The first route is a simple welcome page and acts as our default route. The next route is our orders page. Finally, we have the order-detail page. It is defined by the following pattern: 'orders/:id'. The colon and ID part of the expression are considered a wildcard and representing a parameter in the URL fragment pertaining to the ID of the order. Also notice we have set the 'nav' property to false, as this route will not be part of the menu. This also means that we don't have a static 'href' property provided, as this 'href' is dynamic.

We have configured our router; let's look at the order-detail view model and see how it handles the ID wildcard:

```
export class OrderDetails {

  constructor() { }

  activate(params, routerConfig) {
    this.id = params.id;
    // load order details by provided id
  }
}
```

As you can see, dealing with dynamic routes is very straightforward. We are given a 'params' object that we can grab the 'id' parameter supplied by the route.

Let's look at the orders view to see how this works:

```
<template>
  <section>
    <h1>Customer Orders</h1>
    <a href="#/orders/5">ACME Order 5</a>
  </section>
</template>
```

Although this is arbitrary, it provides a good example of how you can test your own dynamic routes.

Let's take a look at the application with the added routes (Figure 3-2).

Routing	Page 1	Page 2	Page 3	Orders

Customer Orders

ACME Order 5

Figure 3-2. *Orders*

Figure 3-3 shows a single A tag that will load our order-details page.

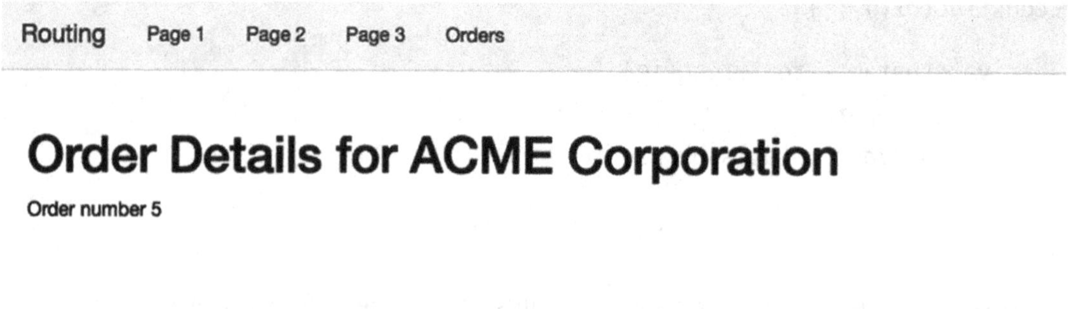

Routing	Page 1	Page 2	Page 3	Orders

Order Details for ACME Corporation

Order number 5

Figure 3-3. *Order details*

The order-details page loads based on the passed-in 'param'. Here is what the order-details.html file looks like:

```
<template>
  <section>
    <h1>Order Details for ACME Corporation</h1>
    <p>
      Order number ${id}
    </p>
  </section>
</template>
```

As you can see, we are simply echoing out the 'id' param that was provided by the 'activate' function.

Child Routers

It is possible to nest your router and configure it as your requirements dictate. The nice thing about the Aurelia router is that it automatically supports nesting without any ceremony. You simply configure your router as you would a top-level router. Let's take a look at what this would look like in the child-router.js view model:

```
export class ChildRouter {

  heading = "Child Router";

  configureRouter(config, router) {
    config.map([
      {route: ["", "page1"], moduleId: "src/page1", title: "Page 1", nav: true},
      {route: "page2", moduleId: "src/page2", title: "Page 2", nav: true},
      {route: "page3", moduleId: "src/page3", title: "Page 3", nav: true},
      {route: "orders", moduleId: "src/orders", title: "Orders", nav: true},
      {route: "orders/:id", moduleId: "src/order-details", title: "Order
      Details"},
```

```
      {route: "child-router", moduleId: "src/child-router", title:
      "Child Router", nav: true},
    ]);

    this.router = router;
  }

}
```

As you can see, we handle the child router exactly as we would a top-level router. Let's see how we can create a child router menu in our child-router.html file:

```
<template>
  <require from="./app.css"></require>

  <section class="au-animate">
    <h2>${heading}</h2>
    <div class="child-router col-md-12">
      <div class="col-md-2">
        <ul class="well nav nav-pills nav-stacked">
          <li repeat.for="row of router.navigation" class="${row.isActive ?
          'active' : ''}">
            <a href.bind="row.href">${row.title}</a>
          </li>
        </ul>
      </div>
      <div class="col-md-10" style="padding: 0">
        <router-view></router-view>
      </div>
    </div>
  </section>
</template>
```

We see here that we are using a UL element as our menu. We repeat over the 'router. navigation' property items to create the menu items inside a LI element. Finally, we render the contents of each route using another 'router-view' custom element.

This is all it takes to create a child router with its own contextual menu. The nice thing about this is that you could change the route mappings based on some business requirements so that the user would only see what you want them to have access to.

Figure 3-4 is a simple screenshot of the child-router view in action.

Figure 3-4. *Child router*

We can see from the screenshot that it takes very little coding to support some complex menu scenarios.

View Ports

You may have your application structure such that you want to have multiple locations respond independently when you navigate to a new route. Aurelia supports this by allowing you to use view ports. Let's create a top-level layout where we have an area dedicated to a contextual menu and another area for our content. Consider the child-view-ports.html file:

```
<template>
  <require from="./app.css"></require>

  <section class="child-router">
    <div class="col-md-2">
      <router-view name="menu"></router-view>
    </div>
```

```
    <div class="col-md-10">
      <router-view name="content"></router-view>
    </div>
  </section>
</template>
```

As you can see from the preceding, we don't have a lot of markup to get our layout set up. We are defining two columns and then we have two instances of the 'router-view' custom element. The only new introduction is that we are providing a new view port for each of our 'router-view' elements. Let's see how we target these named view ports in our child-view-ports.js file:

```
export class ChildViewPorts {

  heading = "Child View Ports";

  configureRouter(config, router) {
    config.map([
      {route: ["", "page1"], viewPorts: { menu: { moduleId: "src/child-nav-
      bar" }, content: { moduleId: "src/page1"}}, title: "Page 1", nav: true},
      {route: "page2", viewPorts: { menu: { moduleId: "src/child-nav-bar"
      }, content: { moduleId: "src/page2"}}, title: "Page 2", nav: true},
      {route: "page3", viewPorts: { menu: { moduleId: "src/child-nav-bar"
      }, content: { moduleId: "src/page3"}}, title: "Page 3", nav: true},
    ]);

    this.router = router;
  }

}
```

In this example, we now have a new property introduced in our routes. We are using the 'viewPorts' property. You can see that we reference the names of the view ports as child properties. We have a 'menu' and 'content' entry for each route. The rest of the syntax is just like before; we have 'moduleId' properties that tell the router where to find the corresponding view model. As you can see from the preceding, we are using the same menu view model for all of our routes but different content. Again, this gives us a lot of flexibility and choices when we are creating our overall UI layout strategy. Figure 3-5 is a screenshot of the child-view-ports view in action.

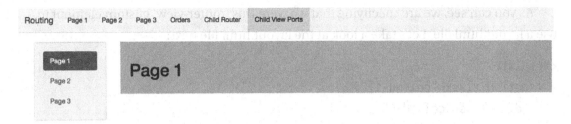

Figure 3-5. *Child view ports*

View ports give us another option when trying to find the best fit that matches our business requirements and user experience.

Layouts

Another powerful option for defining our UI layout is to use the "layout" set of attributes available on the 'router-view' custom element. This approach offers the most control as we can bind to view, view model, and model. The following is a breakdown of each attribute:

- layout-view – identifies the name of the view file to use in the layout

- layout-view-model – identifies the name of the view model file to use in the layout

- layout-model – defines a model parameter that is passed to the view model's activate function

Consider the following child-layout.html file:

```
<template>
  <div>
    <router-view layout-view="src/layout.html"></router-view>
  </div>
</template>
```

As you can see, we are specifying that we want this 'router-view' custom element to use a layout.html file. Let's take a look at the layout.html file next:

```html
<template>
  <section class="col-md-12">
    <div class="col-md-6">
      <slot name="left-content"></slot>
    </div>
    <div class="col-md-6">
      <slot name="right-content"></slot>
    </div>
  </section>
</template>
```

Since we only specified a layout-view attribute in our 'router-view' custom element, we only need to have this file available. As you can see from the preceding, we are simply creating a layout template where we want our content to be injected. Also notice how we are using the SLOT element with the name attribute. This is what you would need to share with any consumer of this layout, as these are the two layout locations where content can be placed.

Let's go back to our child-layout.js file and see how we have our router configured:

```js
export class ChildLayout {

  heading = "Child Layout";

  configureRouter(config, router) {
    config.map([
      {route: "", moduleId: "src/layout-home", title: "Layout Home",
      nav: true},
    ]);

    this.router = router;
  }

}
```

Here, we have a single route pointing to a 'layout-home' view model. We know from the layout.html file where we can inject content; let's take a look and see what is contained in the layout-home.html and see how it is set up:

```
<template>
  <div slot="left-content">
    <p>${leftMessage}.</p>
  </div>
  <div slot="right-content">
    <p>${rightMessage}.</p>
  </div>
  <div>This will not be displayed in the layout because it is not contained
  in any named slot referenced by the layout.</div>
</template>
```

In this markup, we are adhering to the contract as defined by the layout.html file. We are referencing the slots using the slot attribute. Next, we simply use the string interpolation syntax to render the 'leftMessage' and 'rightMessage' properties off of the layout-home.js view model. Notice that we also have another DIV element in our markup. It will not be rendered as it does not target a valid layout location.

Let's look at the layout-home.js file:

```
export class LayoutHome {

  constructor() {
    this.leftMessage = "I'm content that will show up on the left";
    this.rightMessage = "I'm content that will show up on the right";
  }
}
```

This view model simply sets two strings to be rendered in the corresponding layout locations. Figure 3-6 shows how this all comes together.

Figure 3-6. Layouts

Although we only have an example where we are setting the layout-view, it is possible to also set the layout-view-model and layout-model.

With layouts, you should have all of your bases covered as you create your own applications and need a sophisticated layout.

Redirecting Routes

We have already seen how we can create a default route by specifying an empty string ("") , but it is also possible to redirect routes in our route mapping. Consider the following example:

```
config.map([
  { route: "", redirect: "welcome" },
  { route: "welcome", name: "welcome", moduleId: "src/welcome" }
]);
```

As you can see, we have two routes defined. If the user navigates to an empty route, then he/she will be redirected to the "welcome" route.

Unknown Routes

There are times that you might want to map unknown routes to an existing view and view model. This can be handy when users try to navigate to routes where they are not authorized or the route does not exist. The following is an example of a router configuration where we identify an unknown route:

```
import 'jQuery';
import 'bootstrap';

export class App {

  configureRouter(config, router) {
    config.title = 'Routing';
    config.map([
      {route: ["", "page1"], moduleId: "src/page1", href: "#/page1", title:
      "Page 1", nav: true},
```

```
    {route: "page2", moduleId: "src/page2", href: "#/page2", title:
    "Page 2", nav: true},
    {route: "page3", moduleId: "src/page3", href: "#/page3", title:
    "Page 3", nav: true},
    {route: "orders", moduleId: "src/orders", href: "#/orders", title:
    "Orders", nav: true},
    {route: "orders/:id", moduleId: "src/order-details", title: "Order
    Details"},
]);

    config.mapUnknownRoutes("src/unknown-route");

    this.router = router;
  }

}
```

As you can see from the preceding, we simply need to add a call to the function, mapUnknownRoutes, to let the router know where to navigate when an unknown route is encountered. Besides passing in a string, it is also possible to provide a routeConfig object or a function that takes in a NavigationInstruction object for determining what route should be displayed.

Fallback Route

You will encounter scenarios when your application starts up and navigation is rejected for some reason or another. When this happens Aurelia tries to redirect the router to the previous route. This works fine in the middle of a workflow, but if this is the start of the application your users can have a bad experience. To handle for this, you can provide a call to the fallbackRoute function. Consider the following example:

```
import 'jQuery';
import 'bootstrap';

export class App {

  configureRouter(config, router) {
    config.title = 'Routing';
```

```
  config.map([
    {route: ["", "page1"], moduleId: "src/page1", href: "#/page1",
    title: "Page 1", nav: true},
    {route: "page2", moduleId: "src/page2", href: "#/page2", title:
    "Page 2", nav: true},
    {route: "page3", moduleId: "src/page3", href: "#/page3", title:
    "Page 3", nav: true},
    {route: "orders", moduleId: "src/orders", href: "#/orders", title:
    "Orders", nav: true},
    {route: "orders/:id", moduleId: "src/order-details", title: "Order
    Details"},
]);

  config.mapUnknownRoutes("src/unknown-route");
  config.fallbackRoute("src/welcome");

  this.router = router;
 }

}
```

In this example we simply make a call to the "welcome" route whenever the redirect route does not exist.

Summary

The Aurelia router is an extremely powerful and flexible tool. As you build more and more applications, you will come to admire the design behind the routing mechanism and all of the capabilities it brings to the table. There are a lot of features and moving parts with the router. Take some time to play with the capabilities of the router. Don't be afraid to try different scenarios; you will be surprised just how nice it is.

CHAPTER 4

Security and Pipelines

In Chapter 3, we took a look at the capabilities of the router in Aurelia. In this chapter, we are going to take a look at pipelines and how we can use them to enforce security. After completing this chapter, you will have a solid understanding of pipelines and how they work with the router as well as how to enforce your own security for routes in your applications.

Router Pipelines

The router in Aurelia is extremely powerful as we have already seen in the previous chapter. We actually used two different router classes in the previous chapter. There is an AppRouter class that is the overall application router, and then there is the Router class that is used for all child routers. The biggest difference between these two classes is that the AppRouter adds support for pipelines.

Let's take a second and understand exactly what pipelines are and how they work with the router. The router has defined slots where pipelines can interact with the router. The following is a listing of the named slots and when they are called by the router:

- authorize – this is called when loading a route's step but before calling the view model's canActivate function, if it exists

- preActivate – this is called after the view model's canActivate function, if it exists, and the previous view model's deactivate function, if it exists

- preRender – this is called after the view model's activate function, if it exists and the view is rendered

- postRender – this is called after the view has rendered

© Matthew Duffield 2018
M. Duffield, *Practical App Development with Aurelia*, https://doi.org/10.1007/978-1-4842-3402-0_4

If you wish to add a pipeline for any of the slots, you would call it as follows:

- addAuthorizeStep(step)

- addPreActivateStep(step)

- addPreRenderStep(step)

- addPostRenderStep(step)

The step referenced in each of these calls must implement a run function that takes in a navigationInstruction and next parameter.

Authorize Step

Let's set up a simple router with three pages and add an authorize step. Consider the following app.js:

```
import "jQuery";
import "bootstrap";
import {AuthorizeStep} from "./authorize-step";

export class App {
  static inject = [AuthorizeStep];

  constructor(authorizeStep) {
    this.authorizeStep = authorizeStep;
  }

  configureRouter(config, router) {
    config.title = "Pipelines";
    config.addAuthorizeStep(this.authorizeStep);
    config.map([
      {route: ["", "page1"], moduleId: "./page1", href: "#/page1",
      title: "Page 1", nav: true},
      {route: "page2", moduleId: "./page2", href: "#/page2", title:
      "Page 2", nav: true},
```

```
    {route: "page3", moduleId: "./page3", href: "#/page3", title:
      "Page 3", nav: true, settings: { adminOnly: true }},
  ]);

  this.router = router;
  }

}
```

We have added a couple of things to our router. First, we are injecting into our constructor an instance of the AuthorizeStep class. Next, we see that we use this instance and make a call to the addAuthorizeStep off of the config object and pass in our authorizeStep class property. Finally, if you look at the route for 'page3', you will notice that we attached more information in the form of a 'settings' property. We are basically stating that this route should be allowed for admins only.

Let's take a look at how this is enforced in our AuthorizeStep class:

```
import {Redirect} from "aurelia-router";
import {SecurityService} from "./security-service";

export class AuthorizeStep {
  static inject = [SecurityService];

  constructor(securityService) {
    this.securityService = securityService;
  }

  run(navigationInstruction, next) {
    if (navigationInstruction.getAllInstructions().some(i => i.config.
    settings.adminOnly)) {
      if (!this.securityService.isAdmin) {
        return next.cancel(new Redirect(""));
      }
    }
    return next();
  }
}
```

In this example, we are injecting a SecurityService instance that would represent the user security permissions. This could be pulled from a Web API call or some other authentication method. Next, we are implementing the only function required for a pipeline step, the run function. In this function, we are only concerned with routes that expressly want to enforce adminOnly. Remember that this was set on the 'page3' route. If we find a route that returns true, then we check to see if our currently authenticated user is an administrator. Otherwise, we redirect the user back to the default route. This could be a login page or whatever your business requirements dictate.

For completeness, let's look at the SecurityService class:

```
export class SecurityService {

  userId;
  userName;

  constructor() {
    this.isAdmin = false;
  }
}
```

As you can see, this service is very simple. It would be very easy to use a service like this to hold onto a user's state and keep track of their permissions after they have authenticated.

Figure 4-1 shows our application after clicking the Page 3 route.

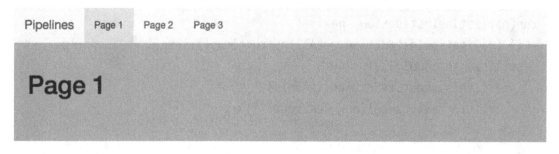

Figure 4-1. *Authorize step*

As you can tell, the router did not allow us to go to the 'page3' route. Instead, it redirected us to the default route, 'page1.'

Audit Step

Now that we have our pipeline set up and are able to check every route to determine if the user has permissions to access it, consider some other uses of these pipelines. It would be easy to instrument in a single pipeline step all user activity regarding navigation with the router. You could save all user navigation activity to a database, for instance.

The following is a simple step that would instrument the user's activity to some back-end service:

```
import {SecurityService} from "./security-service";
import {DataService} from "./data-service";

export class AuditStep {
  static inject = [SecurityService, DataService];

  constructor(securityService, dataService) {
    this.securityService = securityService;
    this.dataService = dataService;
  }

  run(navigationInstruction, next) {
    const options = {
      userId: this.securityService.userId,
      pageViewed: navigationInstruction.config.route
    };
    this.dataService.audit(options);
    console.log('audit-step', options);
    return next();
  }
}
```

As you can see in the preceding, we are injecting the SecurityService plus a DataService. The DataService is used to facilitate communicating with a Web API back end. Next in the run function, you can see that we are simply calling an audit function on the DataService to record the userId and the route.

Here is how we would set up this pipeline for our router:

```
import "jQuery";
import "bootstrap";
import {AuthorizeStep} from "./authorize-step";
import {AuditStep} from "./audit-step";

export class App {
  static inject = [AuthorizeStep, AuditStep];

  constructor(authorizeStep, auditStep) {
    this.authorizeStep = authorizeStep;
    this.auditStep = auditStep;
  }

  configureRouter(config, router) {
    config.title = "Pipelines";
    config.addAuthorizeStep(this.authorizeStep);
    config.addPostRenderStep(this.auditStep);
    config.map([
      {route: ["", "page1"], moduleId: "./page1", href: "#/page1",
      title: "Page 1", nav: true},
      {route: "page2", moduleId: "./page2", href: "#/page2", title:
      "Page 2", nav: true},
      {route: "page3", moduleId: "./page3", href: "#/page3", title:
      "Page 3", nav: true, settings: { adminOnly: true }},
    ]);

    this.router = router;
  }

}
```

As you can see from the preceding, it is easy to keep your step logic simple and clean. You just add the step to the appropriate named slot and you are off to the races. Figure 4-2 is a screenshot of using the AuditStep after viewing 'page1' and 'page2'.

Figure 4-2. *Audit step*

As you can see from the preceding screenshot, the audit step is tracking every route that the user navigates to.

Summary

In this chapter, we looked at a very powerful feature of the router, pipelines. We examined when we can use them and looked at some examples of where we could enforce security as well as audit user activity. There are many more applications to this feature that you can use. Take some time to play with the feature, as you will find that it will allow you to centralize a lot of logic that you would otherwise need to put into each of your view models.

CHAPTER 5

Dependency Injection

Whenever you first look at a new frontend framework, you typically see a simple single-page application with all the pieces embedded in the same file. This approach works for learning a new framework but soon breaks down as your application gains complexity. Your single page can easily become a monster of a file. Dependency injection (DI) is a tried-and-true approach that helps keep your application files small and clean. It also helps mitigate tight coupling and aids with testing.

Most modern frameworks or languages now support some form of dependency injection. In ECMAScript 2015, we were introduced the concept of modules. It allows us to import and export definitions inside our files. This is not a new idea as we have been using a form of module loaders for quite some time. We even have very popular, if not old, formats like CommonJS and AMD. We have used libraries like RequireJS to help load our files. We have even gone so far now as to have bundling libraries like Webpack. These libraries all help with keeping our code small and reducing the footprint of files that need to be loaded for our applications.

Dependency injection is a way for us to bring in dependencies in other files or libraries when we are creating an instance of our classes. In this chapter, we are going to be focusing on dependency injection from a JavaScript perspective and how it is handled within Aurelia. The concept across libraries will be pretty much the same, although the implementation details might differ slightly.

Dependency Injection in Aurelia

Aurelia provides several ways to handle dependency injection in an application. It is possible to actually use the different styles in separate files. If you are developing your application in TypeScript, you even have another more succinct alternative. Let's take a look at a simple example of dependency injection.

51

© Matthew Duffield 2018
M. Duffield, *Practical App Development with Aurelia*, https://doi.org/10.1007/978-1-4842-3402-0_5

Manual Injection

Consider the following app.js file:

```
import 'jQuery';
import 'bootstrap';

export class App {

  message = 'Hello World!';
}
```

In this file we have a simple App class and we have a 'message' property that contains the string 'Hello World!'. Here is the app.html file:

```
<template>
  <h1>${message}</h1>
</template>
```

As you can see these two files should be straightforward. When the view renders, we should simply see the text, 'Hello World!', as shown in Figure 5-1.

Hello World!

Figure 5-1. *Hello World!*

Let's say we want to modify our app.js file so that it injects another class as a singleton, globals.js:

```
export class Globals {
  message = 'Hello Everybody!';
}
```

This is a simple class that we will now inject into our app.js file. We do this as shown in the following example:

```
import 'jQuery';
import 'bootstrap';
import {Globals} from './globals';
```

```
export class App {
  static inject = [Globals];

  message = '';

  constructor(globals) {
    this.globals = globals;
    this.message = this.globals.message;
  }
}
```

Notice that we are importing the newly created Globals class. We are using a path that is relative to our app.js file location. This is important as you may find that your files are not importing correctly if you pass an invalid path. Figure 5-2 is a sample error that is using RequireJS as the loader.

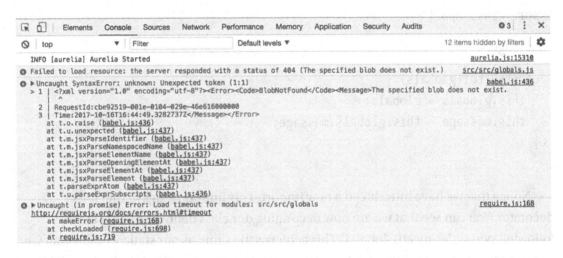

Figure 5-2. *Invalid path*

In our import statement, we used './src/globals'. This is clearly not the relative path for the globals.js file as it is a sibling to app.js. Hopefully this will help you if you run into the same error.

The next thing you should notice is that we are creating the static variable 'inject'. It is this variable that provides us the means to inject the Globals instance into our constructor. This variable can be either a property or a method. It is an array and whatever we put into the array will also need to be delineated in the contructor. Take care that you do not mix the order of your dependencies, as they are managed by order and not by name.

In the constructor, we can provide any name for the dependencies since they are resolved by order and not name.

Let's look at another way in which we can inject our dependencies.

Injection by Decorator

This time, we are going to use a feature known as decorators to accomplish our goal. Consider the app.js file:

```
import {inject} from 'aurelia-framework';
import 'jQuery';
import 'bootstrap';
import {Globals} from './globals';

@inject(Globals)
export class App {

  message = '';

  constructor(globals) {
    this.globals = globals;
    this.message = this.globals.message;
  }
}
```

Notice that we have introduced a new import. This import brings in the 'inject' decorator. You can see that we are now decorating our class definition using the following syntax: '@inject(Globals)'. This achieves the same as our static variable that we used previously. Our constructor does not change in any way and the desired result is exactly the same.

You will need to be sure that you have configured Babel or TypeScript correctly in order to support decorators in your code. If you are using the CLI to create your applications, this has already been done for you.

Autoinjection

If you are developing your application using TypeScript, you have one other alternative to injecting your dependencies that makes it even easier. TypeScript developers will be able to use a new decorator, 'autoinject', in their code. Their app.ts file would look like the following:

```
import {autoinject} from 'aurelia-framework';
import 'jQuery';
import 'bootstrap';
import {Globals} from './globals';

@autoinject
export class App {

  message: string = '';

  constructor(private globals: Globals) {
    this.globals = globals;
    this.message = this.globals.message;
  }
}
```

This time, you see that our code is even more succinct in that TypeScript handles managing the inject property array by analyzing the constructor parameters metadata. TypeScript has enough information to handle the dependency injection for us. If you are using the Aurelia CLI, this capability is already preconfigured, but if you are creating a project manually, you will need to ensure that you set the appropriate compiler options in the 'tsconfig.json' file.

So far, all of your dependencies have been injected as singletons; let's shift gears and look at how we can also inject new instances.

Dependency Injection Containers

As we have seen already, we are able to use dependency injection and inject dependencies as singletons. This means that the exact same instance will go to every class that wants to have the dependency resolved. This may or may not be the desired behavior. For example, you may want to have the 'aurelia-fetch-client' in your application and configure the instance to point to a specific base URL, but there may be one view that needs to pull data from a different URL. How can we tell Aurelia to provide us a new instance of the 'aurelia-fetch-client' instead of the singleton?

Let's take a look at the following code:

```
import {inject, NewInstance} from 'aurelia-framework';
import {HttpClient} from 'aurelia-fetch-client';
import 'jQuery';
import 'bootstrap';
import {Globals} from './globals';

@inject(Globals, NewInstance.of(HttpClient))
export class App {

  message = '';

  constructor(globals, http) {
    this.globals = globals;
    this.http = http;
    // Configure the HttpClient instance...
    this.configureHttpClient();
    this.message = this.globals.message;
  }
  configureHttpClient() {
    //...
  }
}
```

In this example we are using a 'Resolver' in conjunction with our DI container. This resolver, NewInstance, simply tells the DI container that we wish to have a new instance regardless of what the container already has registered. This makes it really easy to have a global instance available in the container but opt to receive a new instance at any time we want.

The preceding example is the most common when you are trying to bring in dependencies from other libraries or from Aurelia itself. As an author, you also have the ability to mark up your classes so that they adhere to a specific lifetime policy. By default, all of our classes will be injected as singletons, but it is possible to decorate our class so that it would always be treated as a new instance, 'transient'. Consider the following example of our Globals class:

```
import {transient} from 'aurelia-framework';

@transient()
export class Globals {
  message = 'Hello Everybody!';
}
```

In the preceding example, we are decorating our Globals class specifying that we want the DI container to always return a new instance whenever it is requested. This gives you, the developer, the option to decide how you want your classes to be resolved via the DI container.

Container Management

It is possible to define all of your container registrations upfront when your application starts. You may have specific requirements where you want to define the object lifetime policy and how the container resolves dependencies in one location instead at each class. You can do this by using the Container API exposed by Aurelia. The API exposes the following methods:

- container.registerSingle(key, classObject) – this allows you to register a class as a singleton. If the key is the same as the classObject, then you are not required to provide the classObject parameter. This is the default behavior that Aurelia does automatically, so it is rarely needed

- container.registerTransient(key, classObject) – this allows you to register a class as a transient. This means that you will get a new instance every time you request the key. If the key is the same as the classObject, then you are not required to provide the classObject parameter

- container.registerInstance(key, instance) – this allows you to register an already configured instance. When you request this key, you will get back the preconfigured instance

- container.registerHandler(key, handler) – this allows you to provide a key and callback function that will be fired every time that you request the key. This may be beneficial for dynamic scenarios where you want your container to provide some custom handling

- container.registerResolver(key, resolver) – this allows you to provide your own resolvers. This means that you can further extend the existing resolvers available in Aurelia with ones that perform operations that are necessary for your application

- container.autoRegister (fn, key) – this allows you to autoregister a type with a particular container. Aurelia performs this seamlessly and returns singleton registrations by default, but you can override this behavior and provide your own

Dependency Injection Resolvers

We have already seen resolvers in action when we looked at the 'NewInstance' resolver. Aurelia provides several resolvers out of the box. The following is a list of resolvers available:

- Lazy – injects a function that lazily evaluates the dependency

- All – injects all of the services registered with a given key. It returns an array of registrations

- Optional – injects an instance of a class only if the class has been already registered in the container

- Parent – instructs the resolution process to skip the current container and perform the lookup on the parent container

- Factory – injects dependencies and allows for passing data to the constructor

- NewInstance – injects a new instance of the dependency regardless of what the container currently has in its registry

Summary

Dependency injection is at the core of developing applications in Aurelia. It provides a great level of abstraction and promotes loose coupling. As you have seen in this chapter, you have a lot of flexibility and options when working with dependency injection in Aurelia. Take some time and play with all of the different options for using DI in your applications. It is only a matter of time until you come across a requirement where using one of the techniques mentioned in the preceding will come in handy.

CHAPTER 6

Services

As your applications become more and more complex, you will find yourself refactoring your code and pulling out redundancies. By using dependency injection (DI), it is easy to create a custom class that corresponds to a set of functions that make it easy to do a specific operation. You will be able to inject your services as singletons or as new instances. This gives you plenty of flexibility to handle all sorts of scenarios in your application.

Creating a service is as simple as exporting a class. What you do in the service depends entirely on what type of functionality you wish to provide. You will find common scenarios such as a data service that wraps the HTTP Client or the HTTP Fetch Client. Configuring an HTTP Client can be redundant across views as well as calling specific Web APIs from your back end. By providing a service that wraps all of this ceremony, you save yourself a lot of work that would otherwise be necessary for every view model.

Consider the following example of getting users from GitHub in the file, github-service.js:

```
import {inject} from 'aurelia-framework';
import {HttpClient} from 'aurelia-fetch-client';

@inject(HttpClient)
export class GithubService {

  users = [];

  constructor(http) {
    this.http = http;

    http.configure(config => {
      config
        .useStandardConfiguration()
```

61

© Matthew Duffield 2018
M. Duffield, *Practical App Development with Aurelia*, https://doi.org/10.1007/978-1-4842-3402-0_6

```
          .withBaseUrl('https://api.github.com/');
    });
  }

  getUsers() {
    return this.http.fetch('users')
      .then(response => response.json())
      .then(data => {
        this.users = data;
      });
  }

}
```

This service uses dependency injection to inject the 'aurelia-fetch-client' into the constructor. It then configures the instance by setting the base URL to 'https://api. github.com'. Finally, it exposes a single function, getUsers. This function performs the call against the GitHub API and fetches 'users'. The response is then set to the property 'users'. Notice that we return the promise from the function. This is important if we were using a router and wanted it to wait during the activation of the view model until the promise is resolved.

Let's see how we use this in our app.js file:

```
import {inject} from 'aurelia-framework';
import {GithubService} from './github-service';

@inject(GithubService)
export class App {

  heading = 'Github Users';

  constructor(svc) {
    this.svc = svc;
  }

  activate() {
    return this.svc.getUsers();
  }
}
```

As you can see from the preceding, we are injecting the GithubService into our constructor using the name 'svc.' Next, in the activate function, we return the promise to the function getUsers. This ensures that if we were using a router, the view would not render until the promise resolved from the getUsers function.

Let's see how to bind to this service in the app.html file:

```
<template>
  <require from="./app.css"></require>
  <require from="./blur-image"></require>

  <section>
    <h2>${heading}</h2>
    <div class="row">
      <div class="col-sm-6 col-md-3 card-container" repeat.for="user of
      svc.users">
        <div class="card">
          <canvas class="header-bg" width="250" height="70" blur-image.
          bind="image"></canvas>
          <div class="avatar">
            <img src.bind="user.avatar_url" crossorigin ref="image"/>
          </div>
          <div class="content">
            <p class="name">${user.login}</p>
            <p><a target="_blank" class="btn btn-default" href.bind="user.
            html_url">Contact</a></p>
          </div>
        </div>
      </div>
    </div>
  </section>
</template>
```

Most of the markup we see in the preceding is related to styling the presentation of the data. Notice that in our repeat.for expression, we are referencing the 'users' array off of the 'svc' object that represents our GithubService instance.

63

Figure 6-1 shows what this would look like in the browser.

Github Users

Figure 6-1. *GithubService*

Depending on your requirements, you could have simply returned the promise in the service instead of exposing an array of 'users.' It all depends on your requirements. For completeness, let's also take a look at the CSS required to render the UI by looking at the app.css file:

```
body {
  margin: 0;
}

.page-host {
  position: absolute;
  left: 0;
  right: 0;
  top: 50px;
```

```css
  bottom: 0;
  overflow-x: hidden;
  overflow-y: auto;
}

section {
  margin: 0 20px;
}

.card {
  overflow: hidden;
  position: relative;
  border: 1px solid #CCC;
  border-radius: 8px;
  text-align: center;
  padding: 0;
  background-color: #337ab7;
  color: rgb(136, 172, 217);
  margin-bottom: 32px;
  box-shadow: 0 0 5px rgba(0, 0, 0, .5);
}

.card .content {
  margin-top: 10px;
}

.card .content .name {
  color: white;
  text-shadow: 0 0 6px rgba(0, 0, 0, .5);
  font-size: 18px;
}

.card .header-bg {
  /* This stretches the canvas across the entire hero unit */
  position: absolute;
  top: 0;
  left: 0;
  width: 100%;
```

```
  height: 70px;
  border-bottom: 1px #FFF solid;
  border-radius: 6px 6px 0 0;
}

.card .avatar {
  position: relative;
  margin-top: 15px;
  z-index: 100;
}

.card .avatar img {
  width: 100px;
  height: 100px;
  -webkit-border-radius: 50%;
  -moz-border-radius: 50%;
  border-radius: 50%;
  border: 2px #FFF solid;
}
```

We won't spend any time on the CSS, but it is a nice reference to review if you are curious how any of the UI was styled.

Summary

Services are a great way to organize your code in a structured manner. It helps keep your code clean and remove redundancies. You have the ability to define your services as singletons, by default, or as transient by simply adding a decorator above your class definition. You will find that you will create several services during your application development as you identify redundancies in your application. As we saw in this chapter, services are simply classes used via dependency injection. You can wrap pretty much any set of functionalities you like and expose them as services. HTTP Client is a perfect example of wrapping up its functionality into a nice clean service to be used by all of your view models.

CHAPTER 7

Getting Data

Most all of your applications are going to require data at some point. Getting data using standard HTTP verbs is easy to use with Aurelia. This makes it very easy to make calls to Web APIs from third parties or hosted within your own network. In this chapter, we are going to take a look at using the HTTP Client, Fetch Client, and interceptors. When you finish this chapter, you will have a good feel for how to get data for your applications.

HTTP Client

We are going to configure a shell for our application that will have elements for a title bar, a side bar for the menu, and finally, an area for the view to be rendered via the router. Consider the screenshot in Figure 7-1.

© Matthew Duffield 2018
M. Duffield, *Practical App Development with Aurelia*, https://doi.org/10.1007/978-1-4842-3402-0_7

Getting Data!

HTTP Client HTTP Fetch Client

Figure 7-1. *Http Client*

In the preceding example, we are using the aurelia-http-client library. Let's take a look at what the view model looks like:

```
import {HttpClient} from 'aurelia-http-client';

export class HttpDataClient {

  constructor() {
    this.http = new HttpClient()
      .configure(x => {
        x.withBaseUrl('https://randomuser.me/');
      });
  }
```

```
activate() {
  this.getUsers();
}

getUsers(numberUsers = 6) {
  let path = `api?nat=us&results=${numberUsers}`;
  return this.http.get(path)
    .then(response => response.content)
    .then(data => this.users = data.results);
  }
}
```

We first import the HttpClient from the 'aurelia-http-client' plug-in. This plug-in is not installed by default, so you will need to execute the following statement using the Aurelia CLI:

```
au install aurelia-http-client
```

Now, you should be able to access the aurelia-http-client plug-in without any errors. We are creating a new instance of the HttpClient and configuring it with a base URL.

It is possible to use dependency injection and inject a singleton of the aurelia-http-client, and this might make sense if you are always going to use the same base URL. Be careful, though, if you are trying to configure to another base URL and you are injecting the singleton. You could inadvertently change the base URL when you only meant to use it for this instance.

In the activate function, we are calling a helper function, getUsers. It allows us to define the number of users we wish to return or defaults to six (6).

We are using the endpoint `http://randomuser.me/` for accessing data. We are setting a path variable that tells the API to only return random users with the nationality set to 'us', and we specify the number of users to return. Next, we make our call use the 'get' HTTP verb. It returns a promise. We are making use of the 'content' property which will format our data by default to JSON. Finally, we return the formatted data to the class-level variable 'users' so that we can bind to the data.

Let's take a look at what our view file looks like. It will actually be the same markup regardless of how we are retrieving our data:

```
<template>
  <require from="./styles.css"></require>

  <div class="users">
    <div class="user" repeat.for="user of users">
      <img src.bind="user.picture.medium">
      <span>${user.name.first} ${user.name.last}
      </span>
    </div>
  </div>
</template>
```

In our markup, we are bringing in a reference to our 'styles.css' file. We then are formatting the results where we have a container DIV element with another DIV that represents each individual user returned in our collection. Next, we use IMG and SPAN elements to present our image and name of the user.

Here is the CSS file for consistency:

```
.users {
  display: flex;
  flex-flow: row wrap;
  justify-content: center;
  align-items: center;
  height: 100%;
  background-color: lightgray;
}
.users .user {
  display: flex;
  flex-flow: column;
  flex: none;
  align-items: center;
  background-color: white;
  border-radius: 5px;
  height: 200px;
```

```
  width: 185px;
  padding: 10px;
  margin: 15px;
  box-shadow: 5px 5px 5px black;
}
.users .user img {
  flex: none;
  height: 150px;
  width: 150px;
}
.users .user span {
  flex: none;
  font-size: large;
}
```

Let's now take a look at some of the features provided by the aurelia-http-client plug-in. You have the following functions that make up the API:

- configure – takes in a function that configures the client. Returns an HttpClient

- createRequest – takes in a string for creating a RequestBuilder. Returns a RequestBuilder

- send – takes in a request message and array of RequestTransforms. Returns a promise of type HttpResponseMessage

- delete – takes in a URL. Returns a promise of type HttpResponseMessage

- get – takes in a URL. Returns a promise of type HttpResponseMessage

- head – takes in a URL. Returns a promise of type HttpResponseMessage

- jsonp – takes in a URL and a callback parameter name. Returns a promise of type HttpResponseMessage

- options – takes in a URL. Returns a promise of type HttpResponseMessage

- put – takes in a URL and content. Returns a promise of type HttpResponseMessage

- patch – takes in a URL and content. Returns a promise of type HttpResponseMessage

- post – takes in a URL and content. Returns a promise of type HttpResponseMessage

Each of the following functions that return an HttpResponseMessage send out an HttpRequestMessage, with the exception of the 'jsonp' function, which instead sends out a JSONPRequestMessage.

Let's take a look at the HttpResponseMessage and its properties:

- response – represents the raw content sent from the server

- responseType – the expected response type from the server

- content – represents the content sent from the server based on the responseType. By default, this is JSON

- headers – objects representing the header data

- statusCode – status code from the server

- statusText – status text from the server

- isSuccess – indicates whether the status code is within the success range

- reviver – a function for transforming the raw response content

- requestMessage – reference to the original request message

It is possible to use the aurelia-http-client using a fluent API approach. Consider the following example:

```
import {HttpClient} from 'aurelia-http-client';

export class HttpDataClient {

  constructor() {
    this.http = new HttpClient();
  }

  activate() {
    this.getUsers();
  }
```

```
getUsers(numberUsers = 6) {
  let path = `api?nat=us&results=${numberUsers}`;
  return this.http.createRequest(path)
    .asGet()
    .withBaseUrl('https://randomuser.me/')
    .send()
    .then(response => response.content)
    .then(data => this.users = data.results);
  }
}
```

The preceding example will work exactly the same as the original code version. You are free to pick and use the style you like the most. Here are the functions that you can chain:

- asDelete()

- asGet()

- asHead()

- asOptions()

- asPatch()

- asPost()

- asPut()

- asJsonp()

- withUrl()

- withBaseUrl()

- withContent()

- withParams()

- withResponseType()

- withTimeout()

- withHeader()

- withCredentials()

- withReviver()

- withReplacer()

- withProgressCallback()

- withCallbackParameterName()

HTTP Fetch Client

Let's now shift gears and take a look at the aurelia-fetch-client. Before using this plug-in, be sure to install it using the following Aurelia CLI command:

```
au install aurelia-fetch-client
```

Figure 7-2 is a screenshot of the calling the same URL endpoint now using fetch.

Getting Data!

Figure 7-2. *Http Fetch*

Let's take a look at what the view model looks like:

```
import {HttpClient} from 'aurelia-fetch-client';

export class HttpDataFetch {

  constructor() {
    this.http = new HttpClient()
      .configure(x => {
        x.withBaseUrl('https://randomuser.me/');
      });
  }

  activate() {
    this.getUsers();
  }

  getUsers(numberUsers = 6) {
    let path = `api?nat=us&results=${numberUsers}`;
    return this.http.fetch(path)
      .then(response => response.json())
      .then(data => this.users = data.results);
  }
}
```

You will notice that the differences between the aurelia-http-client and aurelia-fetch-client are very subtle. We configure the base URL basically the same way. Notice that we use the 'fetch' function off of the http variable to make our request. You will find that this pattern will be the same for all HTTP verbs.

We won't look at the view, as it is exactly the same with the previous markup.

By default, fetch requests use the GET verb. We can override what verb to use using the following syntax:

```
getUpdateUser(user) {
    return this.http.fetch('users',
      {
        method: 'post',
        body: json(user)
      });
  }
```

Notice how we are serializing the body as JSON. This is important as the Fetch API does not have an easy way of sending JSON to the body. The step is simple but it must not be forgotten. The 'json' function we are using is a helper coming from aurelia-fetch-client.

Limitations to Fetch

Take note that if you wish to use the Fetch API on an older browser that doesn't support it, you will need to install a polyfill. The aurelia-fetch-client does not include a polyfill, so it is up to you to ensure that you have this provided when targeting browsers that have not yet implemented the Fetch API.

If you need to support JSONP, use the aurelia-http-client. Currently the aurelia-fetch-client does not support JSONP.

The Fetch also does not support aborting or specifying request timeouts. You also are not able to report progress using a fetch request.

Interceptors

It is possible to hook into requests and responses for both libraries. This allows us to perform some powerful, centralized processing of all actions with our clients. Consider the following HTTP Client interceptor:

```
import {HttpClient} from 'aurelia-http-client';

export class HttpDataClient {

  constructor() {
    this.http = new HttpClient()
      .configure(x => {
        x.withBaseUrl('https://randomuser.me/');
        x.withInterceptor({
          request(message) {
            console.log(`Requesting ${message.method} ${message.url}`);
            return message;
          },
          requestError(error) {
```

```
            console.error(`Request error`, error);
            throw error;
          },
          response(message) {
            console.log(`  Received ${message.statusCode}
            ${message.content.results.length}`);
            return message;
          },
          responseError(error) {
            console.error(`Response error`, error);
            throw error;
          }
      });
    });
  }

  activate() {
    this.getUsers();
  }

  getUsers(numberUsers = 6) {
    let path = `api?nat=us&results=${numberUsers}`;
    return this.http.get(path)
      .then(response => response.content)
      .then(data => this.users = data.results);
  }
}
```

Now you can intercept every request and response and perform any business logic appropriately. This is handy if you want to enforce business policy for access to certain endpoints of data or specific HTTP verbs. Figure 7-3 shows the output from the console:

```
Requesting GET api?nat=us&results=6                              http-data-client.js:29
  Received 200 6                                                 http-data-client.js:37
```

Figure 7-3. *Http Client interceptor console*

For consistency, let's look at how we define our interceptor for our fetch client:

```
import {HttpClient} from 'aurelia-fetch-client';

export class HttpDataFetch {

  constructor() {
    this.http = new HttpClient()
      .configure(x => {
        x.withBaseUrl('https://randomuser.me/');
        x.withInterceptor({
          request(request) {
            console.log(`Requesting ${request.method} ${request.url}`);
            return request;
          },
          requestError(error) {
            console.log(`Request Error`, error);
            throw error;
          },
          response(response) {
            console.log(`  Received ${response.status} ${response.url}`);
            return response;
          },
          responseError(error) {
            console.log(`  Response Error`, error);
            throw error;
          }
        });
      });
  }

  activate() {
    this.getUsers();
  }

  getUsers(numberUsers = 6) {
    let path = `api?nat=us&results=${numberUsers}`;
    return this.http.fetch(path)
```

```
      .then(response => response.json())
      .then(data => this.users = data.results);
  }
}
```

We have a request and response interceptor. Again, we are able to perform any business logic we wish before continuing with the request or response. Figure 7-4 is an example of the output from the console.

```
Requesting GET https://randomuser.me/api?nat=us&results=6          http-data-fetch.js:11
  Received 200 https://randomuser.me/api?nat=us&results=6           http-data-fetch.js:19
```

Figure 7-4. *Http Fetch interceptor console*

Summary

Building a web application is not complete without providing data. In this chapter, we walked you through the two main plug-ins provided by Aurelia for dealing with data. We also took a look at how to intercept requests for each implementation. You should now have the knowledge to allow you to create applications that are able to get data or communicate with HTTP endpoints with very little effort. Just remember that each implementation is unique; your business requirements may dictate which one is best to use for your scenario.

CHAPTER 8

Data Binding

In this chapter we are going to cover how data binding works in Aurelia. We will look at binding data as well as binding events. Upon completing this chapter, you will have a good understanding of how binding works in Aurelia.

Data Binding and Event Binding

Aurelia has a simple binding paradigm. Wherever you see the dot (.) notation in your HTML, you will know that you are looking at a binding syntax. Aurelia treats binding data and events exactly the same way, which makes learning the paradigm very easy and adds to the consistency of the overall framework.

Binding

When building web applications in HTML and JavaScript, getting data to be in sync between your view and your view model has always been a pain. Whether you used jQuery or Knockout or hand-rolled your own solution, it required a lot of ceremony to make sure everything was in sync. Aurelia's binding engine does all of the heavy lifting while still being unobtrusive. You are able to bind to any property you expose in your view model. Let's take a look at the various types of bindings available with Aurelia.

Types of Binding

The following are the various types of data binding with Aurelia:

- one-time – data flows from the view model to the view only once. This is useful for scenarios where you know that the data will never change for the life of the application

```
<a href.one-time="homeUrl">
```

© Matthew Duffield 2018
M. Duffield, *Practical App Development with Aurelia*, https://doi.org/10.1007/978-1-4842-3402-0_8

- one-way – data only flows from the view model to the view but will
  update any time the data changes in the view model

  ```
  <a href.one-way="newsUrl">Latest News</a>
  ```

- two-way – data flows in both from the view model to the view and
  from the view to the view model. This is the most common scenario
  when you want to capture user input from the view

  ```
  <input type="email" value.two-way="email">
  ```

- bind – this uses two-way binding for form controls; otherwise, it uses
  one-way binding. You can use

  ```
  <input type="password" value.bind="password">
  ```

Note   Typically, you can simply use .bind for most scenarios but if you are writing an application that really needs to be performant, then consider using .one-time for data that doesn't change.

Referencing Elements in Bindings

There may be times when you would simply like to bind to an attribute of another element. You can achieve this using the "ref" syntax. By doing this, you are able to reference the element in the DOM, as shown in the following, but also in your view model:

```
<template>
  <label for="username">Username:</label>
  <input name="username" ref="userNameInput">
  <p>
    Hello ${userNameInput.value}, how are you?
  </p>
</template>
```

As you can see from the preceding example, we are referencing the input control and accessing its value attribute. This is not two-way data binding, as the value of the input never gets persisted to a view model, but this can come in quite handy when you simply want to get access to another element.

Let's move on to form controls and what a sample binding would look like for each.

Input

The input element is by far the most common of the form controls. There are many forms that it can take, but the binding syntax remains relatively the same for most. Let's review the input binding syntax:

```
<template>
  <form>
    <label for="username">Username:</label>
    <input name="username" value.bind="username">
  </form>
</template>
```

Check Box

When you bind with a check box, don't use the value attribute. Instead, use the checked attribute as shown in the following:

```
export class User {
  isActive = false;

  constructor() {
  }
}
```

In the preceding view model, we are exposing a single property "isActive". Now, let's look at our markup:

```
<template>
  <form>
    <label for="isactive">Is Active?</label>
    <input type="checkbox" name="isactive" checked.bind="isActive">
  </form>
</template>
```

It is also possible to bind to an object instead of a primitive value. Consider the following view model:

```
export class ShoppingCart {
  review = [
    {
      id: 1,
      value: "Acme Beach Towell"
    },
    {
      id: 2,
      value: "Acme Sun Screen"
    }
  ];
  purchaseIds = [];

  constructor() {
  }
}
```

Our markup changes slightly to accommodate binding to an object:

```
<template>
  <form>
    <h3>Please review your order:</h3>
    <label repeat.for="item of cart">
      <input type="checkbox" model.bind="item.id" checked.bind="purchaseIds">
      ${item.value}
    </label>
  </form>
</template>
```

When you check an item, it will be included in the purchaseIds array. You can also bind to the whole object instead of just a property off of the object.

If you wish to bind against an array of strings, the syntax reverts back to how you would bind to a standard text input control. Consider the following view model:

```
export class Schedule {
  weekDays = [
    "Sunday",
    "Monday",
    "Tuesday",
    "Wednesday",
    "Thursday",
    "Friday",
    "Saturday",
  ];
  weekSchedule = [];

  constructor() {
  }
}
```

In this view model, we have a simple string array of weekdays. Let's see how we bind to this:

```
<template>
  <form>
    <h3>Please enter your schedule request:</h3>
    <label repeat.for="day of weekDays">
      <input type="checkbox" value.bind="day" checked.bind="weekSchedule">
      ${day}
    </label>
  </form>
</template>
```

As you can see from the preceding, we are binding directly to the "value" attribute. The rest of the binding paradigm remains the same.

Radio

Radio buttons are similar to check boxes with one exception: the attribute name must be the same in order for the selected value among the buttons to be mutually exclusive. Consider the following view model:

```
export class Person {

  firstName = "";
  lastName = "";
  gender = "";
  genderOptions = [
    { display: "Male", value: "male" },
    { display: "Female", value: "female" }
  ];

  constructor() {
  }
}
```

Here we see that we have a simple Person view model where we are exposing several properties for binding. We want to expose the gender property to use a set of radio buttons so that when selected the appropriate value is persisted. Let's look at the corresponding view:

```
<template>
  <form>
    <h3>Customer Registration</h3>
    <label for="firstName">First Name:</label>
    <input name="firstName" value.bind="firstName">
    <br />
    <label for="lastName">Last Name:</label>
    <input name="lastName" value.bind="lastName">
    <br />
    <label repeat.for="item of genderOptions">
      <input type="radio" name="genderOption" model.bind="item.value"
      checked.bind="gender">
      ${item.display}
```

```
    </label>
  </form>
</template>
```

Just like the check box, we can bind to simple primitive values or to objects like the preceding example. Also, if you wish to bind to a string array, you will bind against the "value" attribute. Just remember that you must have the same "name" attribute in order for the radio buttons to work together.

Select

The select control allows you to perform either a single selection from a list or multiple selections from a list. Consider the following view model:

```
export class Person {

  firstName = "";
  lastName = "";
  favoriteColor = "";
  colors = [
    "red",
    "green",
    "blue"
  ];

  constructor() {
  }
}
```

We want to bind out select control to the list of colors and allow the user to make a single selection. Let's take a look at the following view:

```
<template>
  <form>
    <h3>Customer Registration</h3>
    <label for="firstName">First Name:</label>
    <input name="firstName" value.bind="firstName">
    <br />
```

```
      <label for="lastName">Last Name:</label>
      <input name="lastName" value.bind="lastName">
      <br />
      <label>
        What's your favorite color?<br/>
        <select valuel.bind="favoriteColor">
          <option value="">Choose...</option>
          <option repeat.for="color of colors" value.bind="color">
            ${color}
          </option>
        </select>
      </label>
    </form>
</template>
```

In this example, we are creating a select control and providing a default empty value. This is convenient if we want our user to select nothing. Next, we are repeating over the colors in the array and binding using the "value" attribute.

Let's look at this same example but using an object instead of a string. Take a look at the following view model:

```
export class Person {

  firstName = "";
  lastName = "";
  favoriteColor = null;
  colors = [
    {id: 1, color: "red"},
    {id: 2, color: "green"},
    {id: 3, color: "blue"}
  ];

  constructor() {
  }
}
```

Now, let's look at how our binding changes slightly:

```
<template>
  <form>
    <h3>Customer Registration</h3>
    <label for="firstName">First Name:</label>
    <input name="firstName" value.bind="firstName">
    <br />
    <label for="lastName">Last Name:</label>
    <input name="lastName" value.bind="lastName">
    <br />
    <label>
      What's your favorite color?<br/>
      <select valuel.bind="favoriteColor">
        <option model.bind="null">Choose...</option>
        <option repeat.for="color of colors" model.bind="color">
          ${color}
        </option>
      </select>
    </label>
  </form>
</template>
```

You will see that binding for selects is very similar to radio buttons and check boxes. This consistency helps especially when learning Aurelia.

Note   Use the same syntax when binding to a multiselect control by including the "multiple" attribute. The rest remains the same with the exception that the "value" property on the select control is expecting an array.

Element Content

There will be times where you want bind to an element that has the "contenteditable" attribute. In this way you will be able to two-way bind to the content of the element. Consider the following view:

```
<template>
  <form>
    <h3>Issue Tracker</h3>
    <label>Description:</label>
    <br />
    <p contenteditable textcontent.bind="description">
    </p>
</form>
</template>
```

In the preceding example, we are simply binding to text but there may be other scenarios where you would rather let the user type in HTML as part of the content. The following is how you would set up your view:

```
<template>
  <form>
    <h3>Issue Tracker</h3>
    <label>Description:</label>
    <br />
    <p contenteditable innerhtml.bind="description">
    </p>
</form>
</template>
```

As you can see from the preceding, we use the "innerHTML" attribute. It's considered a best practice to always sanitize the dynamic HTML that is entered by using the sanitize-html value converter as follows:

```
<p contenteditable innerhtml.bind="description | sanitizeHTML">
</p>
```

Note   Remember that all HTML attributes are converted to lowercase when evaluated. Notice that when we reference objects in our binding expressions, we are now referring to the actual objects in the view model and not what the DOM references. This is an important distinction; the DOM always lowercases all attributes and elements.

Class/Style

Class binding can be achieved either by using string interpolation or using "bind" or "one-time" bindings. Let's look at the following view:

```
<template>
  <h3>Messages</h3>
  <h5 repeat.for="msg of messages" class="${msg.isPriority ? :
  'priority-message' : ''}">
    ${item.display}
  </h5>
</template>
```

In the preceding example, we are adding a class if the underlying "msg" object returns truthy for the "isPriority" property. The following is how you would do the same using "bind":

```
<template>
  <h3>Messages</h3>
  <h5 repeat.for="msg of messages" class.bind="msg.isPriority ? :
  'priority-message' : ''">
    ${item.display}
  </h5>
</template>
```

Finally, here is the "one-time" example:

```
<template>
  <h3>Messages</h3>
  <h5 repeat.for="msg of messages" class.one-time="msg.isPriority ? :
  'priority-message' : ''">
    ${item.display}
  </h5>
</template>
```

If you find that you are dealing with multiple CSS classes, then consider providing a property on your view model to return the correct CSS class in your binding or string interpolation. This will keep your markup clean and mitigate unnecessary business logic in the UI.

Style binding can be achieved by binding to the "style" attribute to either a string or an object. It is recommended to use the "css" attribute instead in order to support Internet Explorer and Edge.

The following is a sample view model with both string and object representations of a style:

```
export class Person {

  firstName = "";
  lastName = "";
  styleString = "background-color: darkgreen; color: white;";
  styleObject = {
    'background-color': cornsilk,
    color: black
  };

  constructor() {
  }
}
```

Before we move to the view, you can see that we are simply imitating what the CSS would look like in a style sheet. Now, let's look at some sample markup:

```
<template>
  <form style.bind="styleString">
    <h3>Customer Registration</h3>
    <label for="firstName">First Name:</label>
    <input name="firstName" value.bind="firstName">
    <br />
    <label for="lastName">Last Name:</label>
    <input name="lastName" value.bind="lastName">
</form>
</template>
```

And binding to an object would look like the following:

```
<template>
  <form style.bind="styleObject">
    <h3>Customer Registration</h3>
    <label for="firstName">First Name:</label>
    <input name="firstName" value.bind="firstName">
    <br />
    <label for="lastName">Last Name:</label>
    <input name="lastName" value.bind="lastName">
</form>
</template>
```

In both scenarios, we are using the exact same syntax. It's best to try and affect your DOM using Classes but if necessary this becomes a very useful tool.

Conditionals

There are two key Aurelia custom attributes that are very powerful when creating a great user experience. They are "if.bind" and "show.bind". Consider the following snippet:

```
<template>
  <form>
    <h3>Customer Registration</h3>
```

```
<label for="firstName">First Name:</label>
<input name="firstName" value.bind="firstName">
<br />
<label for="lastName">Last Name:</label>
<input name="lastName" value.bind="lastName">
<br />
<label>
  Marital Status:
  <select valuel.bind="maritalStatus">
    <option model.bind="null">Choose...</option>
    <option repeat.for="status of maritalStatusValues" model.
    bind="status">
      ${status.display}
    </option>
  </select>
</label>
<br />
<div if.bind="status == 'married'">
  <label for="spouseFirstName">Spouse First Name:</label>
  <input name="spouseFirstName" value.bind="spouseFirstName">
  <br />
  <label for="spouseLastName">Spouse Last Name:</label>
  <input name="spouseLastName" value.bind="spouseLastName">
</div>
  </form>
</template>
```

In the preceding example, we are using the "if.bind" conditional to toggle the presence of the "div" in the DOM. If we were to use the "show.bind" syntax, the "div" would be hidden using an Aurelia CSS class, "aurelia-hide".

Note   Take care when using either the "if.bind" or "show.bind", as each has its own cost and effects. The former adds and removes children from the DOM, which can be expensive, but the latter could also be expensive if you have a large portion of the DOM hidden but all of the bindings are still being updated.

Binding Scopes

Aurelia gives you the ability to set a binding scope using the "with" attribute. This comes in handy if you have an object that you are trying to bind properties and you don't want to type in the parent object multiple times. Let's take a look at sample view model:

```
export class Person {

  currentItem = {
    firstName: "",
    lastName: ""
  };

  constructor() {
  }
}
```

In this class, we have a "currentItem" object as well. We do this to keep our data separate from the rest of the class properties. Let's see how we can use "with.bind" to remove redundancies in our typing:

```
<template>
  <form with.bind="currentItem">
    <h3>Customer Registration</h3>
    <label for="firstName">First Name:</label>
    <input name="firstName" value.bind="firstName">
    <br />
    <label for="lastName">Last Name:</label>
    <input name="lastName" value.bind="lastName">
</form>
</template>
```

Reviewing the preceding markup, we see that we have declared a binding scope on the form element and that anything inside the form will be able to set its bindings in the context of the "currentItem".

Looping

We have already seen looping in several of the preceding coding samples, but let's formally cover it here. You have the ability to repeat any HTML element, including custom elements and templates. We use the "repeat.for" syntax in Aurelia for repeating elements. Consider the following view model:

```
export class Person {

  firstName = "";
  lastName = "";
  favoriteColor = null;
  colors = [
    {id: 1, color: "red"},
    {id: 2, color: "green"},
    {id: 3, color: "blue"}
  ];

  constructor() {
  }
}
```

In our view model we have an array of color objects. Now, let's take a look at the view:

```
<template>
  <form>
    <h3>Customer Registration</h3>
    <label for="firstName">First Name:</label>
    <input name="firstName" value.bind="firstName">
    <br />
    <label for="lastName">Last Name:</label>
    <input name="lastName" value.bind="lastName">
    <br />
    What is your favorite color?
    <label repeat.for="item of colors">
      <input type="radio" name="colorChoice" model.bind="item.id" checked.
      bind="favoriteColor">
```

```
    ${item.color}
  </label>
 </form>
</template>
```

In our view, we see that we are repeating a label for each color that we have in our colors array. We can repeat over primitive arrays as well as ES2015 Maps and Sets.

Value Converters

Value converters are very similar to binding behaviors in syntax. You use the pipe (|) syntax inside a binding expression to identify a value converter. The purpose of a value converter is to allow you to convert a value to a specific format coming from either the view or the view model.

The following is an example of using a value converter in your application:

```
<template>
  <require from="./time-ago"></require>

  last modified ${modifiedDateTime | timeAgo'}
</template>
```

Please refer to Chapter 15 for a deeper understanding of using value converters.

Binding Behaviors

Binding behaviors are used in a binding expression to affect the outcome of the binding. We use the "&" symbol in the binding expression to identify the behavior. You can also pass parameters to behaviors by first providing the name of the behavior followed by a colon (:) and the parameter value. This can be repeated for as many parameters as the behavior expects.

The following is an example of using the "debounce" binding behavior:

```
<input value.bind="search & debounce">
```

Please refer to Chapter 16 for a deeper understanding on using binding behaviors.

DOM Events

As with binding to data, we also the ability to bind to DOM events. The syntax is the same using the event name followed by the dot (.) notation and then the type of binding you wish to use. We will cover the different types of bindings next.

Types of Binding

In Aurelia, we have three different ways to handle events with bindings:

- delegate – this is the suggested approach as it offers the best performance. With event delegation, handlers are not placed on individual elements but placed at a top-level element like the "body". Next, when an event is fired, it "bubbles" up to the top-level handler and then is delegated to the correct element handler based on the target

- trigger – this places an event handler on the individual element. This can incur a performance cost, especially if you have a trigger handler wired up inside a repeating element

- call – this gives you the ability to pass function reference to be called at a future point in time

Delegate

The following is an example of a "save" that will be wired up with the click.delegate:

```
export class Person {
  save(e) {
    // perform save...
  }
}
```

Let's now look at what the view would look like:

```
<template>
  <form>
    ...
```

```
  <button click.delegate="save($event)">Save</button>
  </form>
</template>
```

In the preceding view, we are wiring up the click event using the "delegate" keyword.

Trigger

We will use the same view model as before. Let's look at what the view would look like:

```
<template>
  <form>
    ...
    <button click.trigger="save($event)">Save</button>
  </form>
</template>
```

In the preceding view, we are wiring up the click event using the "trigger" keyword.

Call

Let's assume we have created a custom element and we want to expose a click event on it. We could do so using something like the following syntax:

```
<template>
  <require from="my-element"></require>

  <form>
    ...
    <my-element click.call="handleClick(args)">Save</button>
  </form>
</template>
```

Inside our custom element, we would respond to some business logic that would ultimately execute the function reference passing any parameters the custom element wants. This is extremely powerful and we will see an example of this in Chapter 13.

Summary

We have covered a lot of ground here. It will take some time to become familiar with data binding in Aurelia but it is very consistent and this helps with the learning curve. Don't be afraid to play around with concepts you learned here and try it in your own views and view models.

CHAPTER 9

Templates

In this short chapter we are going to cover ES2015 template strings and their role in Aurelia. We will look specifically at string interpolation and requiring dependencies. Upon completing this chapter, you should have a solid understanding around templates.

Templates

In HTML, we have the <template> element. We use this element to define any markup that we want to be rendered by the Aurelia templating engine. Aurelia follows the standards around using templates and it makes it really easy to use. Let's consider a simple example of a template:

```
<template>
  <h1>Hello World</h1>
</template>
```

This is considered a static template as it simply emits the markup without any bindings. Although this is a simple example, it reinforces the unobtrusive attitude of Aurelia. You are able to use the knowledge you acquired with the standards and then use said knowledge in your development. Let's move on to an example that's a little more complicated.

String Interpolation

ES2015 introduced us to template strings and string interpolation. Everything you learned with string interpolation applies to Aurelia. You use the exact same syntax, which keeps things simple. Consider the following example:

```
<template>
  <h1>Hello ${name}, how are you doing?</h1>
</template>
```

© Matthew Duffield 2018
M. Duffield, *Practical App Development with Aurelia*, https://doi.org/10.1007/978-1-4842-3402-0_9

In this example, we have created a template that has a single string interpolation reference to a property called "name". When Aurelia renders this template, it will examine the corresponding view model to find a property called "name" and emit its value in place of the markup. If you happen to change the value of the "name" property later on, the template will be updated with the new value.

Let's take a look at another example that has both string interpolation and data binding:

```
<template>
  <label>Please enter you name?</label>
  <input value.bind="name">
  <hr />
  <p>Hello ${name}, how are you doing?</p>
</template>
```

As we look at the preceding code sample, we see something that is new. It might not be familiar, as this syntax only belongs to Aurelia. The dot (.) notation identifies anything that will be used in the binding engine with Aurelia. Although this is new, it is still very straightforward, and you will find that it will be very easy to learn. Aurelia allows you to use the dot (.) notation with pretty much all attributes on an HTML element.

If we were to run the preceding sample, we would see that as soon as we start typing in the input, the change would be reflected in the paragraph element below.

Conditional Expressions

You can also put conditional expressions in your string interpolation markup. This provides a lot of flexibility when you are building your template, as you can have it respond to properties off of your view model at runtime and dynamically change. Consider the following template:

```
<template>
<p>You have accessed your account ${accessAttempts} ${accessAttempts > 1 ?
'times' : 'time'}.</p>
</template>
```

Conditional expression inside your string interpolation can provide some very nice features in your application with very little coding.

Note   Take care not to use conditional expressions for everything in your markup. You will find that exposed computed properties may help with keeping your logic centralized in your view model.

Let's move on to yet a little more complicated scenario.

View Resource Pipeline

You will find that as you begin writing your applications in Aurelia, you will create custom elements for code reuse and encapsulation. By creating a custom element, you will be able to reuse it multiple times in the same template and also across multiple pages. The logic and behavior that you code into the custom element will be repeated across all instances.

Let's imagine that we want to create a welcome HTML page that references the preceding code example. We give this example the name "name-tag". Now let's create a new template and reference the "name-tag" custom element.

```
<template>
  <require from="./name-tag"></require>
  <h1>Welcome to Acme Incorporated</h1>
  <p>Please fill out the information below:</p>

  <name-tag></name-tag>
</template>
```

Again, we are using the same template syntax. We have introduced a new element called "require". It is through this element that the Aurelia templating engine resolves dependencies and resources. The "require" simply states that it wants to use the "name-tag" custom element in the template. We then simply use the custom element by its referenced name inside our markup.

Note   We use the "require" tag to bring in custom elements as well as CSS. You would simply do the following for CSS: <require from="./welcome.css"> </require>. The same is true if you have a view with no view model; you would do the following: <require from="./name-tag.html"></require>

We have covered most of the basic scenarios when dealing with templates in Aurelia. There is one more concept that we need to cover that is not new to Aurelia, as it is part of the DOM standard.

Slots

Slots are part of the Shadow DOM specification. They are used to declare two separate DOM trees that can be merged together to produce a single visual rendered result. Consider the following example:

```
<template>
  <div class="panel">
    <div class="panel-header">${header}</div>
    <div class="panel-body">
      <slot name="panelBody"></slot>
    </div>
  </div>
</template>
```

We have created a simple "panel" custom element and we have marked it using a slot so that any consumer of the custom element knows that they can provide their own content. Consider how a developer would use the "panel" custom element:

```
<template>
  <require from="./panel"></require>
  <require from="./name-tag"></require>
  <panel>
    <div slot="panelSlot">
      <h1>Welcome to Acme Incorporated</h1>
      <p>Please fill out the information below:</p>

      <name-tag></name-tag>
    </div>
  </panel>
</template>
```

This should give you a good feel as to the power of the templating engine in Aurelia. Again, the learning curve should be minimal, as most of what we are presented belongs to a standards specification. Aurelia has been very careful to stay as close to the standards as possible when exposing its API.

Composition

There might be times where you would really like to use one template when a certain condition is true but another template when the condition fails. This is possible using the "compose" custom element provided by Aurelia. Consider that we have three separate templates we have created to handle for a greeting in the morning, afternoon, and evening. We will call them "morning", "afternoon", and "evening", correspondingly. In our "welcome" template, we want to be sure to call the correct template based on the time. We could easily have a method that is called "getTemplate()", and all it does is create a new instance of a Date object and determine the correct time and return the name of the correct template. Here's what our template would look like:

```
<template>
  <compose view.bind="getTemplate()"></compose>
</template>
```

You have the ability to bind not only to the "view" but also to the "view model" and "model" attributes on the "compose" custom element.

"as-element" Attribute

There are certain scenarios where HTML can be extremely rigid and it just doesn't want you to put your markup where you want. The Table element is one of those candidates where it doesn't like to have any other content except the exact elements it expects. This can be cumbersome if you are trying to build a library of reusable custom elements and you want to include table rows and columns. Not to worry, Aurelia has a mechanism to support this scenario. You use the "as-element" attribute on the element you want to have the contents swapped out with the view referenced in the attribute. Let's look at an example:

```
<template>
  <td>First column></td>
  <td>Second column></td>
</template>
```

Now, let's look how we will use the "tr-view" view with our "table-view":

```
<template>
  <require from="./tr-view"></require>
  <table>
    <tr as-element="tr-view"></tr>
  </table>
</template>
```

This feature was added mainly due to the way browsers are inconsistent with how they render certain HTML elements. By using this convention, we get a consistent solution that works across browsers.

Summary

Templates are the heart and soul of defining how we want our view rendered. We have learned a lot of new techniques and we will look at several of the features further in later chapters. Aurelia allows you to have full control with regard to how complex your templates become. Start simple and work your way to more advanced scenarios. You will be pleasantly surprised with how powerful Aurelia's templating engine is and how it handles your markup.

CHAPTER 10

Forms and Validation

Most web applications at one point or another will require data entry, and Aurelia has
a very nice validation plug-in that helps reduce the complexity required with ensuring
your forms are enforcing your business rules. In this chapter, we will take a look at
using forms in Aurelia as well as the aurelia-validation plug-in. Upon completing this
chapter, you should have a good understanding of building forms in Aurelia along with
validation.

HTML Form Element

Creating pages that allow users to enter data is fairly straightforward. We use the FORM
element and then provide INPUT elements or other user data entry elements as our
layout. Let's look at the following simple-form.html file:

```
<template>
  <form submit.delegate="submit()">
    <div class="form-group">
      <label class="control-label" for="first">First Name</label>
      <input class="form-control" id="first"
        placeholder="First Name"
        value.bind="currentRecord.firstName">
    </div>
    <div class="form-group">
      <label class="control-label" for="last">Last Name</label>
      <input class="form-control" id="last"
        placeholder="Last Name"
        value.bind="currentRecord.lastName">
    </div>
```

© Matthew Duffield 2018
M. Duffield, *Practical App Development with Aurelia*, https://doi.org/10.1007/978-1-4842-3402-0_10

```
    <div class="form-group">
      <label class="control-label" for="email">Email</label>
      <input type="email" class="form-control" id="email"
        placeholder="Email"
        value.bind="currentRecord.email">
    </div>
    <button type="submit" class="btn btn-primary">Submit</button>
  </form>
</template>
```

In this example, we are using Twitter Bootstrap to help us style our user interface a little. You can see that we have a FORM element. We are assigning the submit event to a function on our view model 'submit()'. This will fire whenever we click a button that is of type 'submit'. You can see that we provide exactly that kind of button as the last element on the form. Next, we have three sets of groups that correspond to three different INPUT elements. We are capturing data for 'firstName', 'lastName', and 'email'. Notice that we are binding to a 'currentRecord' object on our view model.

Let's take a look at the view model for this example:

```
export class SimpleForm {

  currentRecord = {
    firstName: "John",
    lastName: "Doe",
    email: "john@doe.com"
  };

  submit() {
    console.log('submitting...');
  }
}
```

As you can see from the preceding, this is a very simple view model. We basically have a single class property that represents our model object, 'currentRecord'. We also have a single function that is fired when we click the submit button.

Figure 10-1 shows the simple-form.

First Name

John	!

Last Name

Doe

Email

john@doe.com

Submit

Figure 10-1. *Simple form*

Let's move on and get our plug-in installed and ready for use.

Aurelia Validation Plug-in

In order to get the aurelia-validation plug-in to work in your application, you first need to install it. You can do this by executing the following command in your terminal window:

```
au install aurelia-validation
```

This should automatically put an entry in your aurelia.json file under the aurelia_ project folder. The entry should look like the following under the dependencies section:

```
{
  "name": "aurelia-validation.js",
  "dependencies": [
    {
      "name": "aurelia-validation",
      "main": "aurelia-validation",
      "path": "../node_modules/aurelia-validation/dist/amd",
      "resources": []
    }
  ]
}
```

Next, you are going to want to update your main.js file to include the plug-in as seen in the following:

```
import environment from './environment';

export function configure(aurelia) {
  aurelia.use
    .standardConfiguration()
    .feature('resources')
    .plugin('aurelia-validation');

  if (environment.debug) {
    aurelia.use.developmentLogging();
  }

  if (environment.testing) {
    aurelia.use.plugin('aurelia-testing');
  }

  aurelia.start().then(() => aurelia.setRoot());
}
```

As you can see from the preceding, we are simply bringing in the aurelia-validation plug-in using the plug-in function off of the aurelia.use object.

We are all set; we can now start creating our first form with validations. Consider the following registration-form.html file:

```
<template>
  <form submit.delegate="submit()">
    <div class="form-group">
      <label class="control-label" for="first">First Name</label>
      <input type="text" class="form-control" id="first" placeholder="First
      Name"
            value.bind="firstName & validate">
    </div>
    <div class="form-group">
      <label class="control-label" for="last">Last Name</label>
      <input type="text" class="form-control" id="last" placeholder="Last Name"
            value.bind="lastName & validate">
```

```
    </div>
    <div class="form-group">
      <label class="control-label" for="email">Email</label>
      <input type="email" class="form-control" id="email" placeholder="Email"
          value.bind="email & validate">
    </div>
    <button type="submit" class="btn btn-primary">Submit</button>
  </form>
</template>
```

You will notice that our form is pretty much the same as the previous simple-form example. This time, however, we are including a binding behavior, 'validate.' It is this behavior that allows us to validate our form. Let's move on to our view model, registration-form.js:

```
import {inject} from 'aurelia-dependency-injection';
import {
  ValidationControllerFactory,
  ValidationController,
  ValidationRules
} from 'aurelia-validation';
import {BootstrapFormRenderer} from './bootstrap-form-renderer';

@inject(ValidationControllerFactory)
export class RegistrationForm {
  firstName = '';
  lastName = '';
  email = '';
  controller = null;

  constructor(controllerFactory) {
    this.controller = controllerFactory.createForCurrentScope();
    this.controller.addRenderer(new BootstrapFormRenderer());
  }

  submit() {
    this.controller.validate();
  }
}
```

```
ValidationRules
  .ensure(a => a.firstName).required()
  .ensure(a => a.lastName).required()
  .ensure(a => a.email).required().email()
  .on(RegistrationForm);
```

You will notice that there are couple of new things happening in our file. Let's take a look at each one.

We start out by importing several resources from the aurelia-validation plug-in. Next, we import a BootstrapFormRenderer. This is used to actually manipulate the FORM element in the DOM. It is specific targeting forms that have been created using Bootstrap. We will take a look at it in a second. We inject an instance of a ValidationControllerFactory. It is used to create our controller. The controller is used to addRenderer and pass in a new instance of the BootstrapFormRenderer. Finally, we use the controller to validate the form in the submit function. You will have also noticed that we are using the ValidationRules object to define our validation rules for the form. Here, we see that we have made the firstName, lastName, and email all required. We also have stated that the email field should be validated as a valid email address. The ValidationRules object has a very nice fluent application programming interface.

Let's now move on to the BootstrapFormRenderer and look at how it is implemented:

```
import {
  ValidationRenderer,
  RenderInstruction,
  ValidateResult
} from 'aurelia-validation';

export class BootstrapFormRenderer {
  render(instruction) {
    for (let { result, elements } of instruction.unrender) {
      for (let element of elements) {
        this.remove(element, result);
      }
    }
```

```
    for (let { result, elements } of instruction.render) {
      for (let element of elements) {
        this.add(element, result);
      }
    }
  }

add(element, result) {
  if (result.valid) {
    return;
  }

  const formGroup = element.closest('.form-group');
  if (!formGroup) {
    return;
  }

  // add the has-error class to the enclosing form-group div
  formGroup.classList.add('has-error');

  // add help-block
  const message = document.createElement('span');
  message.className = 'help-block validation-message';
  message.textContent = result.message;
  message.id = `validation-message-${result.id}`;
  formGroup.appendChild(message);
}

remove(element, result) {
  if (result.valid) {
    return;
  }

  const formGroup = element.closest('.form-group');
  if (!formGroup) {
    return;
  }
```

```
    // remove help-block
    const message = formGroup.querySelector(`#validation-message-${result.
    id}`);
    if (message) {
      formGroup.removeChild(message);

      // remove the has-error class from the enclosing form-group div
      if (formGroup.querySelectorAll('.help-block.validation-message').
      length === 0) {
        formGroup.classList.remove('has-error');
      }
    }
  }
}
```

The purpose of this class is to manipulate the DOM for a Bootstrap form in order to provide visual cues as to when a form is valid or not. This renderer implements three required functions: render, add, and remove. The render function orchestrates rendering by calling both the add and remove functions. The add function simply adds the validation error information, and the remove function simply removes the validation error.

Figure 10-2 shows the registration-form after clicking the submit button on an empty form.

First Name

```
First Name                                                    🔼
```

First Name is required.

Last Name

```
Last Name
```

Last Name is required.

Email

```
Email
```

Email is required.

Submit

Figure 10-2. *Invalid form*

114

If we provide a valid first and last name but invalid email, the screenshot will look like Figure 10-3.

First Name

John

Last Name

Doe

Email

jd.com

Email is not a valid email.

Submit

Figure 10-3. *Invalid email*

Finally, Figure 10-4 shows how our form will look after we provide a valid email.

First Name

John

Last Name

Doe

Email

john@doe.com

Submit

Figure 10-4. *Valid form*

You will find that once you have played around with the Validation Rules object a couple of times, it is pretty easy to ensure that your form is valid. This only touches the surface of the customization and capability that the aurelia-validation plug-in supports. Take some time and review the documentation from the plug-in to learn how to provide even more advanced scenarios.

Summary

In this chapter, we took a look at the aurelia-validation plug-in. We evaluated the steps required to get the plug-in installed and configured to use within an Aurelia application. Finally, we looked at building forms and what was required to provide validation using Twitter Bootstrap for styling. As you can see, the aurelia-validation plug-in provides a lot of capability and power.

CHAPTER 11

View and Component Life Cycles

One of the excellent features about Aurelia as a framework is that it uses convention over configuration throughout. This removes a lot of overhead and ceremony when developing applications but it can also cause some initial confusion as it will appear that magic happens when you are not familiar with the workflow of the framework. In this chapter, we are going to look at both view and component life cycles.

View Life Cycles

When you use the Aurelia router, all of your views will adhere to a set life cycle. We have seen part of this life cycle when we looked at pipelines. Let's take a closer look at what happens to views when navigated to from the router. Aurelia provides hooks within the view life cycle to allow us to influence the outcome. The following are the hooks we can use:

- canActivate(params, routeConfig, navigationInstruction) – provides ability to control whether or not the router can navigate to this view. Simply return a Boolean, a Promise, or a navigation command

- activate(params, routeConfig, navigationInstruction) – provides the ability to perform custom logic before your view is displayed. If you return a Promise, the router will wait until the Promise returns before displaying the view

- canDeactivate() – provides ability to control whether or not the router can navigate away from this view. Simply return a Boolean, a Promise, or a navigation command

© Matthew Duffield 2018
M. Duffield, *Practical App Development with Aurelia*, https://doi.org/10.1007/978-1-4842-3402-0_11

- deactivate() – provides ability to perform custom logic when your view is being navigated away from. If you return a Promise, the router will wait until the Promise returns before navigating way

All of these hooks are optional. It is not necessary to implement a single one.

In your view model, you only need to implement the function and perform your logic to influence how the router will respond. If you had a view that had a FORM element and you wanted to make sure that the form was not dirty before navigating away, you could implement the canDeactivate() function and put your custom logic there. This would then force the user to save their data prior to navigating away.

The level of control you get from the router is extremely flexible, and you should be able to support any business rule when it comes to controlling who can navigate where.

Component Life Cycles

Every component has a consistent and predictable life cycle. This makes it easy to use the life cycle to our advantage by providing custom logic at any hook. Just like the router view life cycle, Aurelia provides hooks within the component life cycle to allow us to influence the outcome. The following are the hooks we can use:

- constructor – the view model's constructor is the first to be called in the life cycle

- created(owningView, myView) – if provided in the view model, this is called next. At this point during the life cycle, the view has been created and both the view and view model are connected to their controller. The created callback, this function, will receive the instance of the owningView. It is this view where the component has been declared. If the component itself has a view, it will be passed as the myView parameter

- bind(bindingContext, overrideContext) – Data binding between the view and view model is performed next. The bind callback, this function, will be invoked at this time. The bindingContext is the context to which this component is bound. The overrideContext contains information used to traverse the parent hierarchy, and is also used to add any contextual properties the component wants to add

- attached() – The component is attached to the DOM next. The attached callback, this function, will be invoked at this time. This is a good place to provide any custom initialization logic

- detached() – At some time in the future, the component may be removed from the DOM. If this happens, the detached callback, this function, will be invoked

- unbind() – After a component has been removed from the DOM the unbind callback will be invoked, if provided. You can use this function to do any cleanup necessary

All of these hooks are optional. It is not necessary to implement a single one. The common scenario is that if you provide a bind function, you will probably want to provide the unbind function for cleanup. Also remember that the order displayed in the preceding is the order in which the component will go through for its life cycle.

Just like the view life cycles, you have a lot of flexibility and power. Take note that a view is considered a component and it will also adhere to the component life cycle. However, a custom element, for example, will not adhere to the view life cycle. This is important as some developers think that their custom element will have a activate() hook, but this will not happen unless the component is also a view used with the router.

Summary

In this chapter, we looked at both the view and component life cycles. We learned about the optional hooks provided for each life cycle. Take some time to play with each to help solidify your understanding as to how each works. You will find that you will end up using these hooks quite a lot during your development workflow. Therefore, it is important to understand and know the order in which things fire in your Aurelia application.

CHAPTER 12

Event Aggregation

Sometimes you have your screen layout in a certain way that data binding alone does not work. Perhaps you have a custom element in one location and a view in another. A common scenario when building out complex screens is to implement a shell that in turn hosts a specific area where the router will render your views. If you wanted to update your shell when a new view is loaded, this can be cumbersome. Luckily, one way to accomplish this is by using the Event Aggregator. We can use the Event Aggregator to send messages across view models and then perform any actions we like. Let's create a simple shell and two views that get loaded via a router. When we load a view, we want to be sure that the title bar of the shell is updated correspondingly. Upon completing this chapter, you will have a good understanding of how Event Aggregation works in Aurelia.

Setting Up Our Shell

We are going to configure a shell for our application that will have elements for a title bar and a side bar for the menu, and finally, an area for the view to be rendered via the router. Consider Figure 12-1.

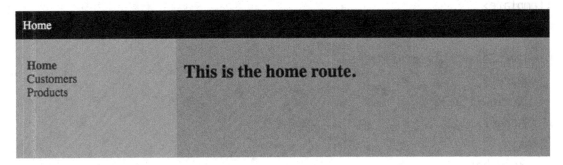

Figure 12-1. *Shell*

© Matthew Duffield 2018

M. Duffield, *Practical App Development with Aurelia*, https://doi.org/10.1007/978-1-4842-3402-0_12

If we click the Customers link, you will notice that the title changes to 'Customers' as well as the area for the router-view changes. You can see this in Figure 12-2.

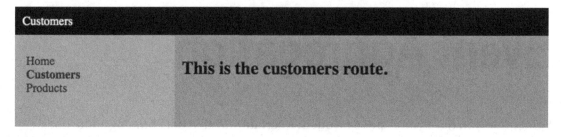

Figure 12-2. *Customers view*

Finally, if we click the Products link, we would see 'Products' in the title and the products information display in the gray region as displayed in Figure 12-3.

Figure 12-3. *Products view*

Now that we have a good idea as how the application works, let's take a look at the app.html file:

```
<template>
  <require from="app.css"></require>

  <div class="holy-grail">
  <header>
    ${viewTitle}
  </header>
  <main>
    <sidebar>
      <ul>
        <li repeat.for="row of router.navigation"
```

```
      class="${row.isActive ? 'active' : ''}">
        <a href.bind="row.href">${row.title}</a>
      </li>
    </ul>
  </sidebar>
  <article>
    <router-view></router-view>
  </article>
  </main>
</div>
</template>
```

We use the app.html file to define our shell regions. We use the header element to identify where we are going to place our title. We also have a sidebar element that we use in conjunction with a ul and repeat over all the routes to create li elements. This is our menu. Next, we have an article element that acts as our host for our routes using the router-view element.

Let's take a look at the app.js file:

```
import {EventAggregator} from 'aurelia-event-aggregator';

export class App {
  static inject = [EventAggregator];

  viewTitle = '';

  constructor(ea) {
    this.ea = ea;
    this.ea.subscribe('active-view', payload => {
      this.viewTitle = payload.title;
    });
  }

  configureRouter(config, router) {
    this.router = router;
    config.title = 'Chapter 12';
    config.map([
      { route: ['', 'home'], name: 'home', moduleId: 'home', title: 'Home',
        nav: true },
```

```
    { route: 'customers', name: 'customers', moduleId: 'customers',
      title: 'Customers', nav: true },
    { route: 'products', name: 'products', moduleId: 'products', title:
      'Products', nav: true },
  ]);
  }
}
```

The following should be fairly straightforward. We are injecting in the EventAggregator. We next configure the EventAggregator to subscribe to the 'active-view' message. We know that the 'payload' will contain a property called "title", and we set our property 'viewTitle' to this value.

The rest of the class simply defines our router. You can see that we have three routes defined: home, customers, and products.

Let's take a look at the home.html file:

```
<template>
  <h1>This is the home route.</h1>
</template>
```

We are more interested in sending and receiving messages in this chapter, so there really is not a lot to see in any of the views.

Let's look at the home.js file:

```
import {EventAggregator} from 'aurelia-event-aggregator';

export class Home {
  static inject = [EventAggregator];

  constructor(ea) {
    this.ea = ea;
  }
  activate() {
    this.ea.publish('active-view', {title: 'Home'});
  }
}
```

Here, you see that this pattern repeats for every view model with the exception that we customize the 'title' to represent the correct view. We could easily extend this by adding other properties that could be used across the application.

The key thing to notice is that we are publishing an 'active-view' message on the EventAggregator instance with a payload. We already saw in the app.js file that we are subscribing for these messages, and when we receive one, we update the class level property accordingly.

The customers and products views are exactly the same with the exception of title.

Manage Your Subscriptions

Whenever we use a resource that lives the life of the application, like the Event Aggregator, it makes sense to manage our subscriptions. The common workflow then is to create an object reference to the subscription like the following:

```
import {EventAggregator} from 'aurelia-event-aggregator';

export class App {
  static inject = [EventAggregator];

  viewTitle = '<View Title>';

  constructor(ea) {
    this.ea = ea;
    this.activeViewSub = this.ea.subscribe('active-view', payload => {
      this.viewTitle = payload.title;
    });
  }
  deactivate() {
    this.activeViewSub.dispose();
  }

  configureRouter(config, router) {
    this.router = router;
    config.title = 'Chapter 14';
    config.map([
```

```
    { route: ['', 'home'], name: 'home', moduleId: 'home', title:
      'Home', nav: true },
    { route: 'customers', name: 'customers', moduleId: 'customers',
      title: 'Customers', nav: true },
    { route: 'products', name: 'products', moduleId: 'products',
      title: 'Products', nav: true },
  ]);
 }
}
```

Notice that we now created a reference to our subscription, 'activeViewSub', in the constructor. Next, we added the 'deactivate' function. When this fires, we simply call 'dispose()' on our subscription reference. If you follow this pattern, you will help ensure that your application manages and uses the Event Aggregator properly. In the preceding example, once you start creating subscriptions inside your view models that are managed by the router, then managing the Event Aggregator becomes more important.

Alternative Approach

Take care when using Event Aggregation, as it is not a magic bullet that should be used for all scenarios. If you can get away with updating UI in different parts of your screen using simple data binding then that should be the recommended approach. One such alternative would be to use a singleton that holds all of the state for the shell part of your screen. In the shell, simply bind the 'title' to the injected instance. Next, in all of the views that are rendered using the router, simply inject the same singleton into the constructors and then update the same property when the view is activated. This will accomplish the same effect but without the overhead of Event Aggregation.

Summary

Although this example may appear simple, you will find scenarios where all you want to do is notify another part of your application of some form of update. This is easily accomplished using the EventAggregator. Remember that if you can update your UI through data binding alone, then don't incur the overhead of using Event Aggregation. However, feel free to play with the Event Aggregator and see its capabilities.

CHAPTER 13

Custom Elements

We have all probably written applications in which we have found ourselves creating the same markup over and over again. Situations like this make for an excellent candidate to create a custom element. In this chapter, we are going to take a look at what it takes to create custom elements, as well as use them in your application. When you finish this chapter, you will have a good knowledge of how to use custom elements in your applications.

What Are Custom Elements?

Let's take a step back and ask ourselves what exactly is a custom element. A custom element is a snippet of HTML that is rendered when the element is referenced. You provide a unique name for your custom element, for example "<my-element></my-element>". When Aurelia encounters a custom element, it tries to see if it can resolve it and render the underlying template used for that custom element. Let's look at the simplest version of a custom element that uses only a view.

Static Custom Elements

In Aurelia, any view can be used as a custom element with or without a view model. Our first custom element will be nothing more than a navigation menu implementation. It will have now behavior and will simply be some static markup bound to a collection of items. In this scenario, we have a router configured with two routes: Page1 and Page2.

© Matthew Duffield 2018
M. Duffield, *Practical App Development with Aurelia*, https://doi.org/10.1007/978-1-4842-3402-0_13

Let's look at the HTML required to create our first custom element:

```
<template bindable="router">
  <nav class="navbar navbar-default navbar-fixed-top" role="navigation">
    <div class="navbar-header">
      <button type="button" class="navbar-toggle" data-toggle="collapse"
      data-target="#skeleton-navigation-navbar-collapse">
        <span class="sr-only">Toggle Navigation</span>
        <span class="icon-bar"></span>
        <span class="icon-bar"></span>
        <span class="icon-bar"></span>
      </button>
      <a class="navbar-brand" href="#">
        <i class="fa fa-home"></i>
        <span>${router.title}</span>
      </a>
    </div>

    <div class="collapse navbar-collapse" id="skeleton-navigation-navbar-
    collapse">
      <ul class="nav navbar-nav">
        <li repeat.for="row of router.navigation" class="${row.isActive ?
        'active' : ''}">
          <a data-toggle="collapse" data-target="#skeleton-navigation-
          navbar-collapse.in" href.bind="row.href">${row.title}</a>
        </li>
      </ul>

      <ul class="nav navbar-nav navbar-right">
        <li class="loader" if.bind="router.isNavigating">
          <i class="fa fa-spinner fa-spin fa-2x"></i>
        </li>
      </ul>
    </div>
  </nav>
</template>
```

Make sure you take note how we are able to bind to the router property. You see that on the template tag, we have a bindable attribute with the value of "router". This is necessary since we do not have a view model for exposing bindable properties. This is a lot of markup that we can now reduce to a single custom element.

Let's look at how we would use this custom element in our app.html file:

```
<template>
  <require from="../styles/styles.css"></require>
  <require from="./nav-bar.html"></require>

  <nav-bar router.bind="router"></nav-bar>

  <div class="page-host" view-spy="">
    <router-view></router-view>
  </div>
</template>
```

Notice that we bring in a reference to the nav-bar.html file using the "require" tag. Next, you can see that we use the "nav-bar" custom element and bind to the "router" property. That is all that is required to get your first static custom element created.

Figure 13-1 shows the custom element in action.

Page 1

Figure 13-1. nav-bar custom element

Let's take what we know and go a step further.

Standard Custom Elements

We have seen that we can reduce a lot of our markup from repeating in our screens by simply taking the redundant parts and creating static custom elements for them. This is a great first step in our journey toward creating a mature toolset to use throughout our application, but we can do so much more. Let's look at creating a multiselector custom element that allows us to select items or remove them through a nice interface. This custom element contains multiple files. Let's get started by looking at the "multi-selector. html" file:

```
<template>
  <require from="./multi-selector.css"></require>
  <require from='./multi-selector-item'></require>

  <div class="multi-selector is-multi is-searchable has-value">
    <div class="multi-selector-control">
      <multi-selector-item repeat.for="item of selectedOptions"
        item.bind="item"
        parent.bind="$parent">
      </multi-selector-item>
      <input ref="dynamicOption"
        spellcheck="false"
        placeholder.bind="placeholder"
        keydown.delegate="processKeydown($event)"
        autocomplete="on"
        class="multi-selector-input"
        list="multi-datalist">
      <datalist id="multi-datalist">
        <option repeat.for="word of options">${word}</option>
      </datalist>

      <span class="multi-selector-clear"
        title="Clear all"
        aria-label="Clear all"
        click.delegate="removeAll($event)">x</span>
    </div>
  </div>
</template>
```

Notice that we are bringing in some CSS to help style our custom element. We are also bringing in a child custom element. This pattern is common when you have a one-to-many relationship that you wish to express in your user interface. You will see that we "repeat" the "multi-selector-item" for every selectedOption. This is the part that shows each individual selection. Next, we will see that we have an input element that is our text entry. This input is wired up to allow for autocompletion, and it uses an HTML 5 feature known as a "datalist". The datalist is the source for our autocompletion. Finally, we have a simple SPAN element that allows us to clear our selection.

Let's see what the view model looks like for this custom element:

```
import {customElement, bindable} from 'aurelia-framework';
import {DOM} from 'aurelia-pal';

@customElement('multi-selector')
export class MultiSelector {
  static inject = [DOM.Element];

  @bindable instanceOptions = [];
  @bindable selectedOptions = [];
  options = [];
  @bindable placeholder = '';

  constructor(element) {
    this.element = element;
  }
  /**
   *  The following is necessary to ensure that we have a unique copy for
      every instance
   *  of our control.
   */
  instanceOptionsChanged(newValue, oldValue) {
    if (this.instanceOptions) {
      this.options = [];
      this.options = [...this.instanceOptions];
    }
  }
  /**
   *  This function performs the selection of an item.
   */
  select(item) {
    this.selectedOptions.push(item);
    this.removeFromOptions(item);
  }
```

```
/**
 *  This function removes a single item from the selectedOptions array.
 */
removeOne(item) {
  let index = this.selectedOptions.indexOf(item);
  this.selectedOptions.splice(index,1);
  this.addToOptions(item);
}
/**
 *  This function removes all items from the selectedOptions array.
 */
removeAll(e) {
  e.stopPropagation();
  for (let i = this.selectedOptions.length - 1; i >= 0; i--) {
    let item = this.selectedOptions[i];
    this.selectedOptions.splice(i,1);
    this.addToOptions(item);
  }
}
/**
 *  This function adds an item to the options array.
 */
addToOptions(item) {
  let index = this.options.indexOf(item);
  if (index === -1) {
    this.options.push(item);
  }
}
/**
 *  This function removes an item from the options array.
 */
removeFromOptions(item) {
  let index = this.options.indexOf(item);
  if (index > -1) {
    this.options.splice(index,1);
```

```
    }
  }
  /**
   * This function handles the keydown event. It checks for the 'enter'
   * key and process the value; otherwise, it simply returns true.
   */
  processKeydown(e) {
    e.stopPropagation();
    if (e.key.toLowerCase() == 'enter' &&
      this.dynamicOption.value.length > 0) {
      this.select(this.dynamicOption.value);
      this.dynamicOption.value = '';
    }
    return true;
  }

}
```

Notice that we start our file with importing "customElement" and "bindable" from the "aurelia-framework". We use the "customElement" reference immediately by decorating our class definition with the name of our custom element. Remember that custom elements are used in HTML and are case insensitive. We change the name of MultiSelector to "multi-selector" as this is how it will be referenced in HTML. The default convention in Aurelia will automatically do this for us, but it is always nice to be consistent with authoring your custom elements.

We next have several properties. We will use these properties to help ensure our custom element works properly. Let's review each:

- instanceOptions – this property holds the list of options to select from

- selectedOptions – this property holds all of the selected options

- options – this property is a list of options to select from but also removes and adds items to the list. It is initialized by the instanceOptions list

- placeholder – this property is a string representation to prompt the user

In our constructor, we are simply injecting the element and keeping for later use.

When we bind to the instanceOptions property, in our own code, we want to be sure that each instance of our custom element gets a unique copy of the data. The select function allows us to add the current item to the selectedOptions list as well as calls a helper function to remove the item from the options list. In our UI, we have the option to remove each item individually or all of them together; this is what the removeOne and removeAll functions handle. The addToOptions function allows you to add an item to the options list. The removeFromOptions does just the opposite by allowing you to remove an item from the options list. Finally, we have a processKeydown function that checks if the user has hit the Enter key and if the INPUT element with a "ref" value of "dynamicOptions" has a length of greater than zero and then adds the value to the selectedOptions list.

Let's take a look at the multi-selector-item.html file:

```
<template>
  <div class="multi-selector-item">
    <span class="multi-selector-item-label">${item}</span>
    <span class="multi-selector-item-icon"
click.delegate="removeOne($event)">x</span>
  </div>
</template>
```

For every item that has been selected, we render the multi-selector-item custom element. This custom element simply displays a label and an icon to allow you to remove the item.

Let's take a look at the view model for this file:

```
import {customElement, bindable} from 'aurelia-framework';

@customElement('multi-selector-item')
export class MultiSelectorItem {
  @bindable item;
  @bindable parent;

  /**
   * This function removes calls the parent view model to removeOne.
   */
```

```
removeOne(e) {
  e.stopPropagation();
  this.parent.removeOne(this.item);
}
```

}

Here we see that we have only one function besides the two bindable properties: item and parent. The removeOne function responds to the click.delegate in the view and calls the parent removeOne function.

Let's look at our last file, multi-selector.css, which is how we are styling our new custom elements:

```css
.multi-selector-control:not(.is-searchable) > .multi-selector-input {
  outline: none;
}
.multi-selector-clear {
  color: #999999;
  cursor: pointer;
  display: inline-block;
  font-size: 16px;
  padding: 6px 10px;
  position: absolute;
  right: 10px;
  top: 0;
}
.multi-selector-clear:hover {
  color: #c0392b;
}
.multi-selector-clear > span {
  font-size: 1.1em;
}

.multi-selector {
  position: relative;
  width: 100%;
}
```

```css
.multi-selector-control {
  position: relative;
  overflow: hidden;
  background-color: #ffffff;
  border: 1px solid #cccccc;
  border-color: #d9d9d9 #cccccc #b3b3b3;
  border-radius: 4px;
  box-sizing: border-box;
  color: #333333;
  cursor: default;
  outline: none;
  padding: 8px 52px 8px 10px;
  transition: all 200ms ease;
  min-height: 34px;
  -webkit-user-select: none;
  -moz-user-select: none;
  -khtml-user-select: none;
  -ms-user-select: none;
  user-select: none;
  width: 100%;
}
.multi-selector-control:hover {
  box-shadow: 0 1px 0 rgba(0, 0, 0, 0.06);
}
.multi-selector.is-multi .multi-selector-control {
  padding: 8px 18px 8px 8px;
}

.multi-selector.is-multi .multi-selector-input {
  margin: 2px;
}

.multi-selector-item {
  background-color: #f2f9fc;
  border-radius: 2px;
  border: 1px solid #c9e6f2;
```

```css
  color: #0088cc;
  display: inline-block;
  font-size: 1em;
  margin: 0 2px 5px 2px;
  padding: 2px;
}
.multi-selector-item-icon {
  cursor: pointer;
  border-bottom-left-radius: 2px;
  border-top-left-radius: 2px;
  border-left: 1px solid #c9e6f2;
  padding: 2px 5px 2px;
}
.multi-selector-item-icon:hover,
.multi-selector-item-icon:focus {
  background-color: #ddeff7;
  color: #0077b3;
}
.multi-selector-item-icon:active {
  background-color: #c9e6f2;
}
.multi-selector-item-label {
  padding-left: 2px;
  padding-right: 4px;
}
}
```

Take a moment to review how the CSS selectors are managing the style of our custom element.

Let's use page2.html and add the multiselector custom element to the markup:

```html
<template>
  <h1 class="">Page 2</h1>
  <form>
    <div class="form-group">
      <label for="flavor">What's your favorite ice cream?</label>
      <multi-selector
```

```
        name="flavor"
        instance-options.bind="iceCreamList"
        selected-options.bind="selectedIceCream"
        placeholder="Select flavor...">
      </multi-selector>
    </div>
  </form>
</template>
```

In this example, we have added a FORM element to our markup. You can tell we are using Twitter Bootstrap to help with styles as well. We have a label and then our custom element. You can see all of our properties from our custom element in action. Let's now look at the view model:

```
export class Page2 {
  iceCreamList = [];
  selectedIceCream = [];

  constructor() {
    this.iceCreamList = [
      "chocolate",
      "strawberry",
      "vanilla"
    ];
  }
}
```

You can see from our view model that we have two properties: iceCreamList and selectedIceCream. We are using the iceCreamList as our instanceOptions list and we are using the selectedIceCream as our selectedOptions list.

Figure 13-2 shows our custom element.

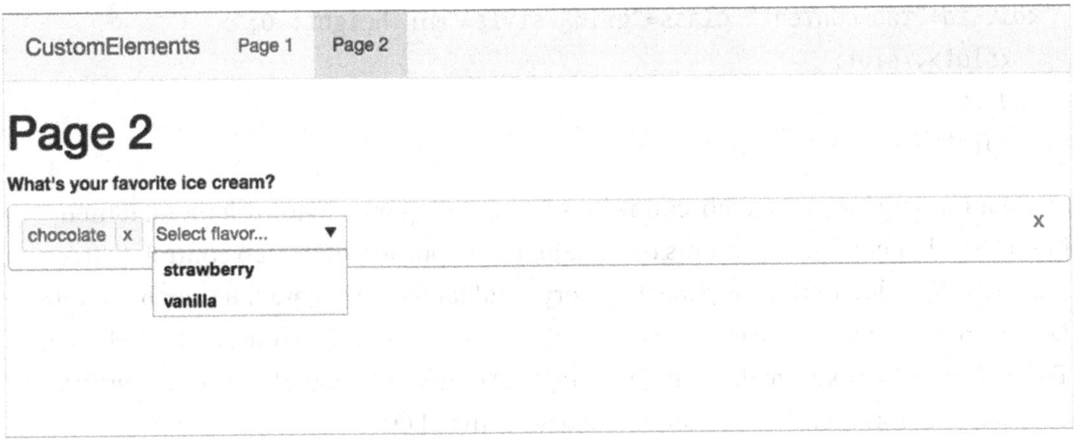

Figure 13-2. *Multiselector custom element*

Let's move on to our final scenario.

Advanced Custom Elements

We have moved from static to standard custom elements and we have seen the advantage each brings to our development toolset. It would be nice to have a custom element that can do everything we have seen as well as manage child elements elegantly. Let's look at creating a tab-control custom element where we will have a tab-control parent as well as tab-item children.

Here is what our tab-control.html file looks like:

```
<template>
  <require from='./tab-control.css'></require>

  <div id="tab-header" class="">
    <span repeat.for="tab of tabs"
      click.delegate="navClick($event)"
      class="${selectedTab === tab.name ? 'active' : ''} ${tab.isVisible ==
      'true' ? '' : 'hidden'}"
      id="${tab.name}">
      ${tab.header}
    </span>
  </div>
```

```
<div id="tab-content" class="grid" style="min-height: 0;">
  <slot></slot>
</div>
</template>
```

Our markup brings in a tab-control.css file to styling our custom element. It then has a DIV element that represents the header or tab portion of the tab control. In it, we create a SPAN element that repeats for every child tab that is created. It then has another DIV element that hosts the content of individual tabs. You will also see a SLOT element. This is where the magic really happens. The SLOT element allows for us to put arbitrary content, and it will render the content instead of the SLOT.

Let's take a look at what our tab-control.js view model looks like:

```
import {customElement, bindable, children} from 'aurelia-framework';
import {DOM} from 'aurelia-pal';
import {EventAggregator} from 'aurelia-event-aggregator';

@customElement('tab-control')
export class TabControl {
  static inject = [DOM.Element, EventAggregator];

  @children('tab-item') tabs = [];
  @bindable selectedTab = 'tab1';

  constructor(element, messageBus) {
    this.element = element;
    this.messageBus = messageBus;
  }

  selectedTabChanged(newValue, oldValue) {
    this.fireSelectionChange();
  }

  attached() {
    let tab = this.tabs.find(f => f.name === this.selectedTab);
    if (tab) {
      tab.selectedTab = this.selectedTab;
      this.fireSelectionChange();
    }
  }
}
```

```
navClick(e) {
  this.selectedTab = e.target.attributes['id'].value;
}

fireSelectionChange() {
  let selectionChangingEvent = DOM.createCustomEvent('selection-
  changing', {bubbles: true, detail: this.selectedTab});
  this.element.dispatchEvent(selectionChangingEvent);
  setTimeout(() => {
    this.tabs.forEach((t) => {
      t.selectedTab = this.selectedTab;
    });
    let selectionChangedEvent = DOM.createCustomEvent('selection-
    changed', {bubbles: true, detail: this.selectedTab});
    this.element.dispatchEvent(selectionChangedEvent);
  }, 25);
  }
}
```

As you can see from the preceding, we are bringing in the same things we have before but there are a couple of new ones. You will notice that we are importing "children" from the aurelia-framework. You will see how we are using these new additions shortly.

We immediately use the "children" decorator to specify that the tabs array will be a collection of tab-item custom elements. We also expose a bindable property for the selectedTab.

In our constructor, we simply set the element and EventAggregator to class-level variables.

Our selectedTab property is bindable, and thus it will fire a change event whenever it changes. The selectedTabChanged function simply calls the fireSelectionChange helper function.

We are using the attached function to let us know when the custom element has been attached to the DOM. It is ready then to handle any UI interactions, and we want to initialize our tab-control with the properly selected tab.

The navClick function is what is called when a user clicks any SPAN element that represents the tab header.

Finally, the fireSelectionChange function defines two custom events: selection-changing and selection-changed. It defines each event to bubble as well as places the selectedTab as the detail of the event. We first dispatch the "selection-changing" event and then iterate over all of the tabs updating each selectedTab property on the tab-item custom element. Lastly, we fire the "selection-changed" event.

Let's take a look at the tab-item.html file:

```
<template class="grid" show.bind="selectedTab === name">
  <slot></slot>
</template>
```

This is pretty simple markup. We add a class to the TEMPLATE element as well as a show.bind construct that basically says only show this custom element when the selectedTab property matches the name property. Finally, it has a SLOT element that allows the user to put any content they want.

Let's look at the tab-item.js view model:

```
import {customElement, bindable} from 'aurelia-framework';
import {DOM} from 'aurelia-pal';

@customElement('tab-item')
export class TabItem {
  static inject = [DOM.Element];

  @bindable name = '';
  @bindable header = '';
  @bindable selectedTab;
  @bindable isVisible = 'true';

  constructor(element) {
    this.element = element;
  }
}
```

As you can see, this is another fairly simple view model. We are only exposing a handful of bindable properties:

- name – this is the name of the tab-item. It must be unique for all other tabs

- header – this is what is displayed in the tab-control

- selectedTab – this is the currently selected tab-item

- isVisible – this determines if the tab-item is visible or not. Recall that this is referenced in the tab-control SPAN element to add or remove the "hidden" class

For completeness, let's take a look at the tab-control.css file:

```css
tab-control {
  display: grid;
  grid-template-rows: auto 1fr;
  position: relative;
}
tab-control #tab-header,
tab-control #tab-content {
  position: relative;
}
tab-control #tab-header {
  border-radius: 5px 5px 0 0;
  line-height: 2.2em;
}
tab-control #tab-header>span {
  position: relative;
  background: #293846;
  background: lightgray;
  color: darkgray;
  border-radius: 5px 5px 0 0;
  padding: .5em;

  cursor: pointer;
  user-select: none;
}
tab-control #tab-header>span.active {
  background: #CC412F;
  color: white;
  margin-left: 5px;
  margin-right: 5px;
}
```

```
tab-control #tab-header>span:hover {
  filter: brightness(65%);
}
tab-control #tab-content {
  margin: 0;
}
tab-item {
  position: relative;
}
```

Take a second to review how we are using the CSS to style our custom elements. Let's now look at page3.html and see how we are using the tab-control:

```
<template>
  <h1 class="">Page 3</h1>
  <tab-control
    selection-changed.delegate="tabSelectionChanged($event.detail)"
    selected-tab="tab1">
    <tab-item name="tab1"
      header="Tab 1">
      <h2>Tab 1 contents....</h2>
    </tab-item>
    <tab-item name="tab2"
      header="Tab 2">
      <h2>Tab 2 contents....</h2>
    </tab-item>
  </tab-control>
</template>
```

Here we see that we are creating our tab-control custom element. We are wiring up the selection-changed event having it call the "tabSelectionChanged" function. We could have also wired up the selection-changing event as well. In these events, we can perform any processing that we need when a tab selection changes. Next, you will see that we have two instances of the tab-item custom element. Each tab-item must have a unique name. You can see that we are referencing which tab is the selected tab by the "selected-tab" attribute on the tab-control custom element. We also provide a header for each tab-item. This is what is displayed for each tab. The contents of each tab-item is what is displayed when you click either tab.

Let's look at the page3.js view model:

```
export class Page3 {

  tabSelectionChanged(detail) {
    if (this.currentTab === detail) return;
    console.log('tabSelectionChanged', detail);
  }

}
```

As you can see, this is a very simple view model. We don't need to do very much processing. We have a function, "tabSelectionChanged", so that we can perform any necessary business logic when a tab changes.

Figure 13-3 shows the final version.

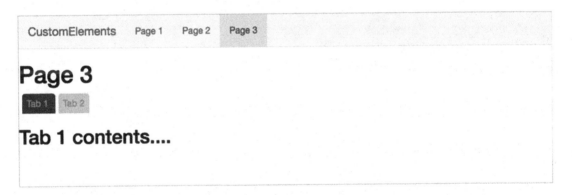

Figure 13-3. *tab-control custom element*

As you can see, our tab-control looks great. We can adjust the CSS however we like to make it look and feel exactly how we want.

Summary

Learning how to build custom elements takes some practice, especially with all of the powerful capabilities Aurelia brings to the table. We went from a simple scenario to two more complex examples of custom elements where there were multiple custom elements working together. You should now be able to weave together your own custom elements to further help reduce redundant code and enrich your own toolbox. Don't be afraid to experiment and try out different custom elements for your business needs.

CHAPTER 14

Custom Attributes

Custom attributes might be considered even more powerful than custom elements. With custom attributes, we have the ability to provide added functionality to existing markup. We don't even need to create new elements; we simply provide our own attribute and it adds unique behavior to the element it was attached to. In this chapter, we are going to create some custom attributes that will help make our development life cycle easier. When you finish this chapter, you will have a solid understanding of what you can do with custom attributes as well as when to use them.

Defining Custom Attributes

You may be curious and wondering exactly what a custom attribute is. A custom attribute is an HTML attribute that is attached to any HTML element. You add custom attributes in all lowercase, following the same convention for custom elements; for example, "<input type='text' set-focus>". Notice that a custom attribute can be assigned information or not. We will look at both examples shortly. Let's get started with our first custom attribute, 'set-focus'.

Set-Focus Custom Attribute

We are going to create a custom attribute that will allow us to identify which element to set focus when the page loads. Typically, this is used in a form for data entry. By creating a set-focus custom attribute, we will be able to reuse this logic and behavior across all of our screens so that we have a consistent code scenario with no redundancies cluttering our view models.

© Matthew Duffield 2018
M. Duffield, *Practical App Development with Aurelia*, https://doi.org/10.1007/978-1-4842-3402-0_14

Let's look at the set-focus.js file:

```
import {customAttribute} from 'aurelia-templating';
import {DOM} from 'aurelia-pal';

@customAttribute('set-focus')
export class SetFocus {
  static inject = [DOM.Element];

  constructor(element) {
    this.element = element;
  }

  attached() {
    this.element.focus();
  }

}
```

As you can see from the preceding code, this is a very simple custom attribute. Basically, we are calling the focus() function off of the element to which the custom attribute is attached.

Let's look at how we would use this custom attribute in our app.html file:

```
<template>
  <require from="./app.css"></require>
  <require from="src/resources/attributes/set-focus/set-focus"></require>
  <section class="page-section">
    <h1>${message}</h1>
    <form>
      <div class="form-group">
        <label for="name">
          Name
        </label>
        <input id="name"
          type="text"
```

```
            value.bind="currentRecord.name"
          set-focus>
      </div>
    </form>
  </section>
</template>
```

We are first bringing in a reference to an "app.css" file so that we can have a little style. Next, we are bringing in our custom attribute. We have a pretty long path that we are dealing with, but we will address that shortly. Now, looking at the markup, we see some standard HTML elements. We see that we have H1 element as well as a FORM element with a single DIV, LABEL, and INPUT. Attached to the INPUT element, we see that we are using the custom attribute. When we run this application, we will notice that the page will load and that focus will be set to the INPUT element.

Figure 14-1 shows the custom attribute in action.

Customer Information

Name

Figure 14-1. *Set-focus custom attribute*

Before we move on, let's remove the dependency of the "require" tag for the custom attribute. The following are the steps required to configure our application to make our custom attributes global.

We first need to create an "index.js" file that will represent all of our custom attributes in our application. Here is what the file should look like:

```
export function configure(config) {
  config.globalResources([
    './attributes/set-focus/set-focus'
  ]);
}
```

This file will be located just inside the "resources" folder in our project structure. Now, we need to update our "main.js" file so that it points to this file. This process is part of what it takes to create a "feature" in Aurelia.

```
export function configure(aurelia) {
  aurelia.use
    .standardConfiguration()
    .developmentLogging()
    .feature('resources');

  aurelia.start().then(a => a.setRoot());
}
```

As you can see from the preceding, we only added ".feature('resources');" to our code. That is a pretty nice convenience making our custom attributes globally available to all of our views.

Input-Mask Custom Attribute

There may be times when you would like to allow your users to input data into a FORM but you would like to constrain what they can type to some form of mask. We are going to create an input-mask custom attribute that will allow us to use Regular Expression to define our mask for input. Let's take a look at the "input-mask.js" file:

```
import {customAttribute, bindable} from 'aurelia-framework';
import {DOM} from 'aurelia-pal';

/**
 *  Name: input-mask
 *  Desc: This is an input mask custom attribute.
 *  Usage: <input class="form-control"
 *  value.bind="currentItem.phone"
 *  input-mask="pattern: (###) ###-####;"
 *  placeholder="(555) 555-1234">
*/
@customAttribute('input-mask')
export class InputMask {
  static inject = [DOM.Element];
```

```
@bindable pattern = ''; // '####-##-##' or '(###) ###-####' or '##:##'

constructor(element) {
  this.element = element;
  if (element instanceof HTMLInputElement) {
    this.element = element;
  } else {
    throw new Error('The input-mask attribute can only be applied on
    Input elements.');
  }
}

attached() {
  this.element.addEventListener("keydown", this.keyDownHandler.
  bind(this));
}
detached() {
  this.element.removeEventListener("keydown", this.keyDownHandler.
  bind(this));
}

keyDownHandler(e) {
  let value = e.target.value;
  let isInt = Number.isInteger(Number.parseInt(e.key));
  let key = e.key.toLowerCase();
  let valueLen = value.length;
  let patternLen = this.pattern.length;
  let char = this.pattern[valueLen];
  let options = {
    e,
    value,
    isInt,
    key,
    valueLen,
    patternLen,
    char
  };
```

```
    let result = true;
    if (this.isValidNonInputKey(key)) {
      // valid key input...
    } else if (valueLen === patternLen) {
      e.preventDefault();
      result = false;
    } else if (char === '#' && isInt) {
      // valid key input...
    } else if (this.processKey(options)) {
      // valid key input...
    } else {
      // bad input...
      e.preventDefault();
      result = false;
    }
    return result;
  }

  processKey(options) {
    let {key, char, isInt, valueLen, e} = options;
    if (key === char) {
      return true;
    } else if (char !== '#' && isInt) {
      let nextChar = this.pattern[valueLen + 1];
      if (nextChar === ' ') {
        e.target.value = e.target.value + char + ' ';
      } else {
        e.target.value = e.target.value + char;
      }
      return true;
    }
    return false;
  }
```

```
isValidNonInputKey(key) {
  let keys = [
    "backspace",
    "arrowleft",
    "arrowright",
    "arrowup",
    "arrowdown",
    "home",
    "end",
    "tab"
  ];
  return keys.includes(key);
}

}
```

We start off by identifying our class as an 'input-mask'. Next, we inject the DOM Element into our constructor. We are also exposing a bindable property, "pattern". It is this property that we will provide a Regular Expression to represent our mask.

Let's look a little more closely at our constructor. We are doing something new here. We are now making sure that we can only put this custom attribute on INPUT elements. If we find that we have this custom attribute on anything other than an INPUT element, we throw an error. This is nice practice, in that it gives a lot of flexibility and control over the definition of our custom attributes. It also gives us an opportunity to provide a meaningful error message to developers who might be using our custom attributes.

In the attached() function, we see that we are adding an event listener to the "keydown" event. We remove the listener in the detached() function.

The keyDownHandler is where our custom attribute begins to work. We begin by taking in the event argument from the keydown event. Since we know that we are dealing with an INPUT element, it is safe for us to access the "value" property of the "target" object. We also check to see if the key typed is an integer. Since you can type upper- and lowercase characters, we arbitrarily lowercase the key value. Next, we check the overall length of what has been typed into the INPUT element as well as the length of the pattern defined in the custom attribute.

We create an options helper hash that holds onto all of the variables we have recently created. We will use this options variable shortly.

Now perform our conditional logic. We first check to see if the key entered is a valid non-input key as defined in the function, isValidNonInputKey(). This function checks to see if the key entered matches any of the keys defined in the "key" array. If it passes then we simply ignore the key press and return true.

If what we have typed into the INPUT element has reached the same length of the pattern, we don't allow any more entries by returning false.

If the current pattern character is a '#' and the key that was typed is an integer, then we simply ignore the key press and return true.

Next, we call a helper function, processKey(), to ensure that our pattern is being adhered to correctly. It first checks if the key entered and the pattern character match. If not, it checks to see if the current pattern character is not an integer but the entered key is an integer. Next, it computes the nextChar value by grabbing the next pattern character. If the next character is a space, it injects the space; otherwise it simply adds the character to the end of the value of the INPUT element and returns true.

Before we take a look at markup, let's update the "index.js" file so that we can make this custom attribute globally available. Here is an updated version of the "index.js" file:

```
export function configure(config) {
  config.globalResources([
    './attributes/set-focus/set-focus',
    './attributes/input-mask/input-mask'
  ]);
}
```

As you can see, we simply added another entry for our input-mask custom attribute.

Let's see this custom attribute being used in our app.html file:

```
<template>
  <require from="./app.css"></require>

  <section class="page-section">
    <h1>${message}</h1>
    <form>
      <div class="form-group">
        <label for="name">
          Name
        </label>
```

```
      <input id="name"
        type="text"
        value.bind="currentRecord.name"
        set-focus>
    </div>
    <div class="form-group">
      <label for="phone">
        Phone Number
      </label>
      <input id="phone"
        type="text"
        value.bind="currentRecord.phone"
        input-mask="pattern: (###) ###-####;"
        placeholder="(555) 555-1234">
    </div>
  </form>
  </section>
</template>
```

We have already seen most of this markup. If you look at the last INPUT element, you will see that we have introduced our custom attribute. The beauty of this custom attribute is that it allows us to pass any mask we want, and then we use the placeholder property of the INPUT element to show the user the mask. This gives us a lot of power. If you were to try and test this view, you would see that you would not be able to type in any character except the ones represented by the pattern.

Notice also that we no longer have any "required" tags pointing to our custom attributes.

Figure 14-2 shows what the input-mask looks like.

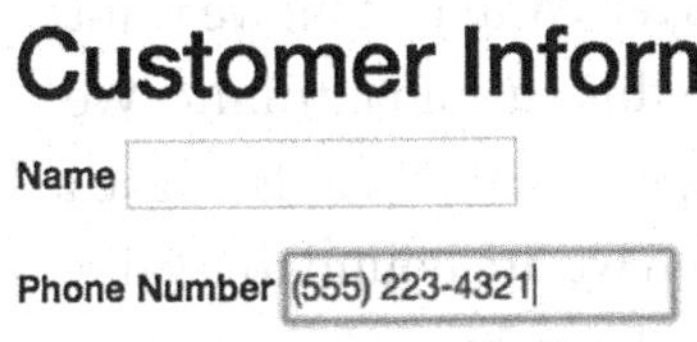

Customer Information

Name

Phone Number (555) 223-4321

Figure 14-2. Input mask

Circle Custom Attribute

This next custom attribute may be contrived, but it shows some more advanced features of custom attributes and how you can use them on your own. Let's consider that we want our users to be able to have a form and type in a color and then render the color in a DIV element with the corresponding color. Sounds great, right? Well, there are a couple of features that we will employ that make this a valuable example.

Consider the following code for the "circle.js" custom attribute:

```
import {bindable, customAttribute} from 'aurelia-templating';
import {DOM} from 'aurelia-pal';

@customAttribute('circle')
export class Circle {
  static inject = [DOM.Element];

  @bindable({ primaryProperty: true }) color;
  @bindable size = 25;

  constructor(element) {
    this.element = element;
    this.element.style = `height:${this.size}px; width:${this.size}px;
border-radius: 15px;`;
  }

  colorChanged(newValue, oldValue){
    this.element.style.backgroundColor = newValue;
  }
}
```

We have seen most of this before, but there are a couple of new additions. First, we see that we are providing a "primaryProperty" property. This tells Aurelia that we want the "color" property to be considered the default property on this custom attribute. We will see how we can use this feature in the markup next. Also, notice that we also have a function "colorChanged". This function is what responds when we are bound to a value that changes. This gives us the ability to make our custom attribute dynamic and allow users to change the "color" of this custom attribute.

Let's now look at how we would use this custom attribute:

```
<template>
  <require from="./app.css"></require>

  <section class="page-section">
    <h1>${message}</h1>
    <form>
      <div class="form-group">
        <label for="name">
          Name
        </label>
        <input id="name"
          type="text"
          value.bind="currentRecord.name"
          set-focus>
      </div>
      <div class="form-group">
        <label for="phone">
          Phone Number
        </label>
        <input id="phone"
          type="text"
          value.bind="currentRecord.phone"
          input-mask="pattern: (###) ###-####;"
          placeholder="(555) 555-1234">
      </div>
      <div class="form-group">
        <label for="color">
          Color
        </label>
        <input id="color"
          type="text"
          value.bind="currentRecord.color">
        <div circle="color.bind: currentRecord.color;">
        </div>
```

```
        </div>
      </form>
    </section>
</template>
```

The part worth evaluating is the last INPUT and DIV elements. You can see that we are binding the "color" of the currentRecord object to the "value" of the INPUT element. Next, we add our "circle" custom attribute to the DIV element and bind it to the same "color" property. If we type "skyblue" in the INPUT element we will see the following (Figure 14-3):

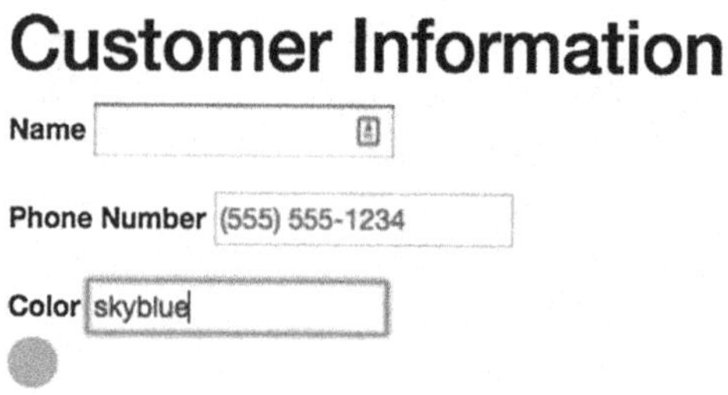

Customer Information

Name [   ]

Phone Number (555) 555-1234

Color skyblue

Figure 14-3. *Using the INPUT element*

Recall that we identified the "color" property to be our default property. This means that we can modify our markup to look like the following and things will still work:

```
<div class="form-group">
  <label for="color">
    Color
  </label>
  <input id="color"
    type="text"
    value.bind="currentRecord.color">
  <div circle.bind="currentRecord.color">
  </div>
</div>
```

As you can see, we can bind the "circle" directly to the default property, which is the "color" in our case. This is just a simple example of the flexibility and conventions available to us as we create our suite of custom attributes.

Summary

Custom attributes complement our existing knowledge of custom elements. These two core features of Aurelia really provide a bulk of the power of creating a rich toolset of reusable components in your development. We looked at some very simple scenarios like setting focus to a FORM element. Next, we moved on to a more advanced input-mask custom attribute that performed more advanced business logic. Finally, we looked at some of the conventions and features of what custom attributes can do as a whole. You should now be armed with enough knowledge to start creating your own rich set of custom attributes. The power of this development model is that you can test these custom attributes thoroughly and know that they will just work in the rest of your views. Take some time to write and create your own custom attributes.

CHAPTER 15

Value Converters

In this chapter we are going to cover how value converters work in Aurelia. We will review the API and conventions that Aurelia uses when working with value converters. We will also create our own value converter. Upon completing this chapter, you will have a good understanding of how value converters work in Aurelia.

Value Converters

Value converters are very similar to binding behaviors in syntax. You use the pipe (|) syntax inside a binding expression to identify a value converter. A value converter is a class that is responsible for converting view model values into values for use in the view and vice versa.

Value converter classes implement the following interface with two functions:

- toView – function used for converting a value to be used in the view
- fromView – function used for converting a value to be used in the view model

You are able to pass multiple value converters using the pipe (|) symbol.

Conventions

Aurelia identifies value converters by looking at your code and finding all classes that have the trailing "ValueConverter" suffix in your class names. As long as you follow this convention, your value converter will be ready to use in your application. When you "require" a value converter, you do not need to provide the suffix; Aurelia is smart enough to look for a class with the same prefix and a "ValueConverter" suffix.

161

© Matthew Duffield 2018
M. Duffield, *Practical App Development with Aurelia*, https://doi.org/10.1007/978-1-4842-3402-0_15

Building Your First Value Converter

We now have a good understanding of the API and conventions. Let's go ahead and create our first value converter. Consider the following class:

```
import moment from 'moment';

export class TimeAgoValueConverter {
  toView(value) {
    return moment(value).fromNow();
  }
}
```

In this class, we are importing MomentJS to help us with formatting. We simply want to create a converter that displays information using the "... ago" syntax.

Let's see what our view would look like using this:

```
<template>
  <require from="./time-ago"></require>

  last modified ${modifiedDateTime | timeAgo'}
</template>
```

In our view model, we are exposing a "modifiedDateTime" property. In our view, we bring in our value converter. Note that we can reference the name of the value converter using the name of the class in all lowercase and hyphens (-) where our camel casing changes. We also do not need to supply the suffix "value-converter", as Aurelia will look it up with proper suffix by convention.

Figure 15-1 shows what our TimeAgo value converter would look like:

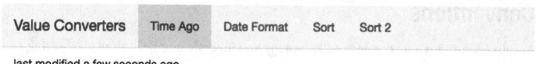

Figure 15-1. *TimeAgo value converter*

Note   You may be wondering why we are referencing the value converter using lowercase and hyphenation. This is because Aurelia is complying with HTML element and attribute specifications.

As you may have guessed, we can also pass parameters to our value converters. Consider the following value converter:

```
import moment from 'moment';

export class DateFormatValueConverter {
  toView(value, format) {
    return moment(value).format(format);
  }
}
```

We use yet another feature of MomentJS to allow for us to format our dates. Let's see how we can format dates in our view:

```
<template>
  <require from="./date-format"></require>

  last modified ${modifiedDateTime | dateFormat:'MMMM D, YYYY'}
</template>
```

As you can see, we are able to create a suite of value converters once and use them across our application in any view we need. If you have multiple parameters, you would repeat using the colon (:) followed by the value.

It is also possible to databind value converter parameters. Consider the following example:

```
<template>
  <require from="./date-format"></require>

  <label for="dateSelect">Select format:</label>
  <select id="dateSelect" ref="dateSelect">
    <option value="MM-DD-YY">MM-DD-YY</option>
    <option value="MM/DD/YY">MM/DD/YY</option>
    <option value="MM-DD-YYYY">MM-DD-YYYY</option>
```

```
    <option value="MM/DD/YYYY">MM/DD/YYYY</option>
</select>

  last modified ${modifiedDateTime | dateFormat:dateSelect.value}
</template>
```

In this example, we see that we have four different formats provided by the select element. We added a "ref" name to the select element so that we could reference it in our binding expression.

Figure 15-2 displays the DateFormat value converter after selecting MM/DD/YYYY as the format in the drop-down:

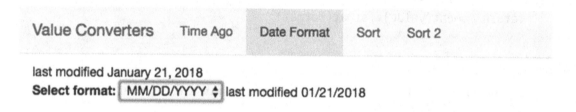

Figure 15-2. *DateFormat value converter*

Multiple Parameters

It is also possible to have your parameters be objects instead of primitives. Let's look at another value converter. This one will provide sort capabilities for a table. Consider the following example:

```
<template>
  <require from="./sortable-table.css"></require>
  <require from="./sort"></require>

  <table class="table table-striped">
    <thead>
      <tr>
        <th click.delegate="sortBy('company')">Company</th>
        <th click.delegate="sortBy('country')">Country</th>
      </tr>
    </thead>
```

```
  <tbody>
    <tr repeat.for="row of rows | sort:columnName:direction">
      <td>${row.company}</td>
      <td>${row.country}</td>
    </tr>
  </tbody>
 </table>
</template>
```

The preceding code sample has a simple table. Notice that we are binding the "click" event of the TH elements. We pass in the name of the column to the "sortBy" function. This function simply handles the logic of setting the "columnName" and "direction", as we will see shortly. You also will see that we are passing two parameters to the SortValueConverter. Finally, you have noticed that we are bringing in a "sortable-table. css" file to handle some simple styling. We will take a look at this as well. Let's look at the "sortable-table.js" file now:

```
export class SortableTable {

  columnName = '';
  direction = '';
  rows = [
    { company: 'Berglunds snabbkop', country: 'Sweden' },
    { company: 'North/South', country: 'UK' },
    { company: 'Alfreds Futterkiste', country: 'Germany' },
    { company: 'Koniglich Essen', country: 'Germany' },
    { company: 'Magazzini Alimentari Riuniti', country: 'Italy' },
    { company: 'Paris specialites', country: 'France' },
    { company: 'Island Trading', country: 'UK' },
    { company: 'Laughing Bacchus Winecellars', country: 'Canada' }
  ];

  sortBy(propertyName, direction) {
    if (this.columnName === propertyName) {
      if (this.direction === 'ascending') {
        this.direction = 'descending';
      } else {
```

```
      this.direction = 'ascending';
    }
  } else {
    this.direction = 'ascending';
    this.columnName = propertyName;
  }
 }

}
```

Looking at the preceding view model, we see that we have declared three variables: columnName, direction, and rows. The rows array is what our table is bound to for creating all the TR elements. We use the columnName and direction properties to support how we are sorting. The sortBy function takes in two parameters: columnName and direction. It uses these two parameters to set our class-level properties: columnName and direction. If you recall, it is these two properties that we are using in our value converter expression.

Let's now move on to the sort.js file:

```
export class SortValueConverter {
  toView(array, propertyName, direction) {
    let factor = direction === 'ascending' ? 1 : -1;
    let newArr = array.sort((a, b) => {
      if (a[propertyName] < b[propertyName]) {
        return -1 * factor;
      } else if (a[propertyName] > b[propertyName]) {
        return 1 * factor;
      }
      return 0;
    });
    return newArr;
  }
}
```

In this value converter, we are taking in an array, propertyName, and direction parameters. We use the propertyName and direction parameters to determine how we use the native sort function off of a JavaScript array. We return the new array, which is used in our binding expression.

Let's quickly look at the sortable-table.css file and review what we have there:

```
.table thead tr th {
  user-select: none;
}
```

You see that we added a simple CSS selector to target our TH elements inside a ".table" class. By doing this we can ensure that we don't select the text of the TH elements, since we wish to use the header as a toggle.

Figure 15-3 shows what the Sort value converter looks like after clicking the Company column:

Value Converters	Time Ago	Date Format	Sort	Sort 2	

Multiple Parameters

Company	Country
Alfreds Futterkiste	Germany
Berglunds snabbkop	Sweden
Island Trading	UK
Koniglich Essen	Germany
Laughing Bacchus Winecellars	Canada
Magazzini Alimentari Riuniti	Italy
North/South	UK
Paris specialites	France

Figure 15-3. *Sort value converter*

Parameters as Objects

In the preceding examples, you have seen where we have set the parameters as either a literal value or referencing properties from the underlying view model. It is also possible to use object literals inline in your binding expression. The following is what it would look like to use a value converter using objects:

```
<template>
  <require from="./sortable-table.css"></require>
  <require from="./sort"></require>

  <table class="table table-striped">
    <thead>
      <tr>
        <th click.delegate="sortBy('company')">Company</th>
        <th click.delegate="sortBy('country')">Country</th>
      </tr>
    </thead>
    <tbody>
      <tr repeat.for="row of rows | sort: {propertyName: columnName,
      direction: direction}">
        <td>${row.company}</td>
        <td>${row.country}</td>
      </tr>
    </tbody>
  </table>
</template>
```

Although you can use this approach, you will lose the ability for Aurelia to track changes on the columnName and direction properties, as these are now copied into a new object. There may be simple scenarios that do not require binding or change tracking, but this would not be one of those cases.

Figure 15-4 demos that tracking is lost when clicking the column header:

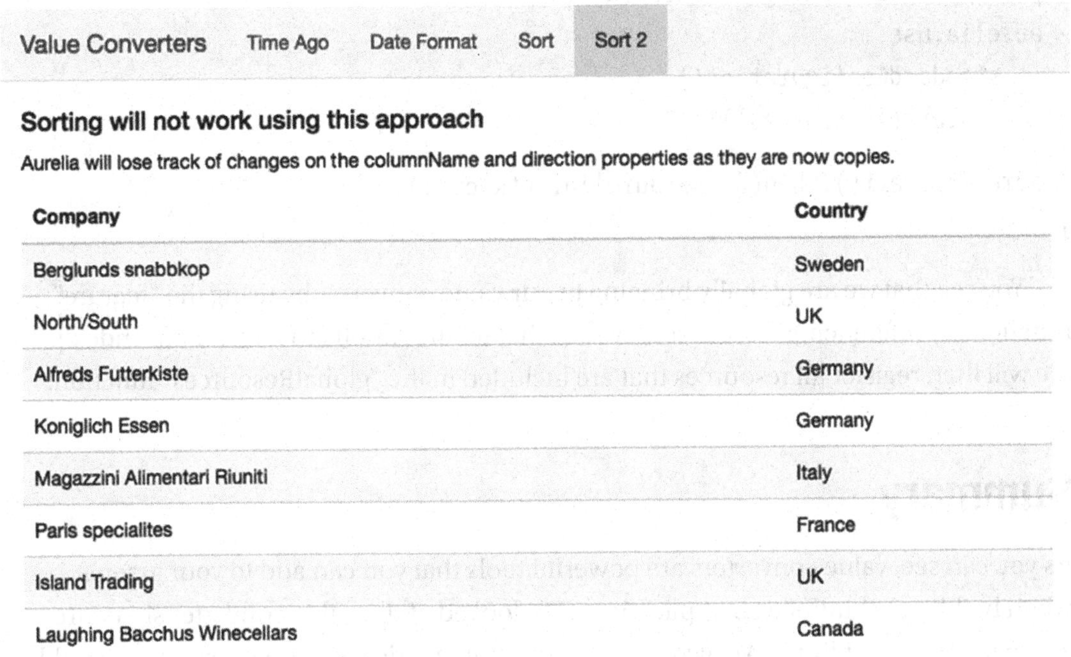

| Value Converters | Time Ago | Date Format | Sort | Sort 2 |

Sorting will not work using this approach

Aurelia will lose track of changes on the columnName and direction properties as they are now copies.

Company	Country
Berglunds snabbkop	Sweden
North/South	UK
Alfreds Futterkiste	Germany
Koniglich Essen	Germany
Magazzini Alimentari Riuniti	Italy
Paris specialites	France
Island Trading	UK
Laughing Bacchus Winecellars	Canada

Figure 15-4. *Sort with tracking lost*

Making Your Value Converters Global

Up until now, we have always referenced our value converters inline in our view markup. It is possible to remove our dependency of using the "require" element and simply reference the value converter. We make use of a "globalResources" function. Using the preceding SortValueConverter example, the following is what an "index.js" file would look like inside the "resources" folder:

```
export function configure(config) {
  config.globalResources([
    './value-converters/sort-value-converter'
  ]);
}
```

The final step we need to do is reference this index file in our "main.js" file:

```
export function configure(aurelia) {
  aurelia.use
    .standardConfiguration()
    .feature('resources');

  aurelia.start().then(() => aurelia.setRoot());
}
```

You see that we are globally bringing in our value converter by using the "feature" function. By referencing "resources," we see that telling Aurelia to look for an "index.js" file will then register all resources that are included in the "globalResources" function.

Summary

As you can see, value converters are powerful tools that you can add to your arsenal when building beautiful web applications. We looked at the value converter signature and naming conventions. We also reviewed several practical examples where we could use value converters in our own applications. Finally, we learned how to reference our resource globally, removing the need to use the "require" element.

CHAPTER 16

Binding Behaviors

In this chapter we are going to look at how binding behaviors work in Aurelia. We will address some of the standard behaviors that come with Aurelia as well as how to create your own custom binding behavior. Upon completing this chapter, you will have a good understanding of how binding behaviors work in Aurelia.

Binding Behaviors

Binding behaviors are used in a binding expression to affect the outcome of the binding. We use the "&" symbol in the binding expression to identify the behavior. You can also pass parameters to behaviors by first providing the name of the behavior followed by a colon (:) and the parameter value. This can be repeated for as many parameters as the behavior expects. You can also mix binding behaviors with value converters in the same binding expression. Aurelia comes with the following binding behaviors:

- throttle – limits the rate at which the view is updated in one-way binding scenarios or limits the rate at which a view model is updated in two-way scenarios. The default throttle value is 200ms

  ```
  <input value.bind="search & throttle">
  ```

  Here is an example of throttling after a half-second:

  ```
  <input value.bind="search & throttle:500">
  ```

- debounce – limits the binding from being updated until after a set time interval has passed without any changes. The default debounce value is 200ms

  Throttle will fire as soon as the limit has been met and then wait for the same limit before firing again automatically

  ```
  <input value.bind="search & debounce">
  ```

© Matthew Duffield 2018
M. Duffield, *Practical App Development with Aurelia*, https://doi.org/10.1007/978-1-4842-3402-0_16

Here is an example debounce after a half-second:

```
<input value.bind="search & debounce:500">
```

In the preceding example, you might have a REST call that performs a request whenever the "search" property changes. This behavior falls closer to what a user would expect when typing and then pausing, as the limit will not be exercised until the last change has been made

- updateTrigger – allows you to override the input events that cause an element's value to be persisted to the view model. The default events are "change" and "input"

```
<input value.bind="search & updateTrigger:'blur'">
```

Here, we have identified that we wish this binding to update on the "blur" event. You can have multiple triggers and do so as follows:

```
<input value.bind="search & updateTrigger:'blur':'paste'">
```

Here, we have identified that we want this binding to update on both "blur" and "paste" events.

- signal – allows you to notify a string interpolation binding to refresh. A common scenario would be showing a user how old a record is. You would use a value converter that would take in the original property and then calculate the passage of time and display it appropriately

```
last modified ${modifiedDateTime | timeAgo & signal:'time-signal'}
```

In the preceding example, we have our "modifiedDateTime" object that we pass through a "timeAgo" value converter to formatting purposes. Finally, we identify that we wish to expose a named signal, "time-signal". The following is how we would trigger this signal from the view model:

```
import {BindingSignaler} from 'aurelia-templating-resources';
```

```
export class Person {
  static inject = [BindingSignaler];

  constructor(signaler) {
    this.signaler = signaler;

    setInterval(() => {
      this.signaler.signal('time-signal');
    }, 3000);
  }
}
```

You see that we are importing the "BindingSignaler" which handles all the orchestration for notifying the correct bindings. It is possible to have multiple signals defined with the same name so that they are updated at the same time. You will find that this scenario will come in handy when you want to update bindings that are not part of your current view model but need to be updated regardless.

Figure 16-1 shows what the screen would look like after that page has just loaded:

Chapter 16 - Binding Behaviors

Signal

last modified a few seconds ago

Figure 16-1. *BindingSignaler initial load*

If we wait a minute, our screen will update to look like the following (Figure 16-2):

Chapter 16 - Binding Behaviors

Signal

last modified a minute ago

Figure 16-2. *BindingSignaler after a minute delay*

- oneTime – allows you to specify a string interpolation binding to only happen once

  ```
  ${title & oneTime}
  ```

This is a great feature, as it helps keep your application running as robustly as possible by mitigating further property observations.

- self – is useful when you are setting up an event binding and only wish for the event to fire on the target element and not on any of its descendants

  ```
  <div>
    <header mousedown.delegate="handleMouseDown($event) & self">
      ${title}
      <button>Close</button>
    </header>
  </div>
  ```

This is extremely useful, as it helps keep our code in our view model clean by not needing to test the target of the event and ensuring that it is truly the "header" that the event is firing on. Previously, we would have needed to test the target passed by the event or used CSS like "user-select: none;" which would not be favorable if you want also handle events from the children.

Custom Binding Behaviors

We have now seen all of the binding behaviors that are available out of the box from Aurelia, but what if you would like to handle a special scenario? This is where Aurelia really shines with its extensibility. Let's pretend that we want to create something similar to the "self" binding behavior. We would like to wire up multiple nested "click.delegate" and only have the innermost child fire. We can easily do this using the "stopPropagation" function off of the event arguments that are passed when the event is fired. Let's take a look at our custom binding behavior called "StopPropagationBindingBehavior":

```
export class StopPropagationBindingBehavior {
  bind(binding, source) {
    binding.standardCallSource = binding.callSource;
    binding.callSource = function(event) {
```

```
      this.standardCallSource(event);
      event.stopPropagation();
    };
  }

  unbind(binding, source) {
    binding.callSource = binding.standardCallSource;
    binding.standardCallSource = null;
  }
}
```

When dealing with writing your own binding behaviors, you will always have two functions that you will need to implement: bind and unbind. We use the "bind" function to wrap our custom logic before calling the underlying bound function. Next, we use the "unbind" function to remove our wrapping and clear out any properties that were used.

This is really nice as it allows us to create just about any logic we want and encapsulate it in a binding behavior for reuse throughout our application.

Let's look at how this is used in our view:

```
<template>
  <require from="./binding-behavior-view.css"></require>

  <div click.delegate="divClick($event)">
    <button click.delegate="buttonClick($event) & stopPropagation">
    Click Me!</button>
  </div>
</template>
```

As you can see, this is very similar to the "self" binding behavior, but it should provide you with enough to start building your toolset of custom binding behaviors for your own application.

Finally, let's look at our view model and see what we are doing in our click event handlers:

```
export class BindingBehaviorView {

  divClick(e) {
    console.log('divClick', e);
  }
```

```
buttonClick(e) {
  console.log('buttonClick', e);
}
}
```

We see that we are simply echoing out that either DIV or the Button element has been clicked. If we were to remove our custom binding behavior and we clicked the Button, we would see both messages in the console. However, when we are using the custom binding behavior, it stops the propagation of the event so that it only fires on the child element.

Figure 16-3 shows the BindingBehaviorView view rendered with the DIV wrapping the Button:

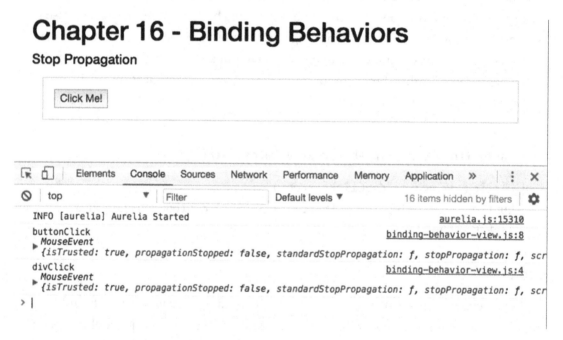

Figure 16-3. *BindingBehaviorView*

As you can see, we first clicked on the Button but propagation stopped and did not continue to the DIV. Next, we clicked the DIV.

Summary

You should now have a good understanding of the available binding behaviors in Aurelia and how to use them. We also looked at how to build our own custom binding behavior. This is yet another powerful capability which comes in real handy when you have requirements that need to be implemented globally across your application.

CHAPTER 17

Compose

We have already covered how to create custom elements, but there might be scenarios where you would like your view to be dynamic based on some given criteria. You might find yourself in scenarios where you would like to render specific views based on user interaction. Let's go with the example that we have a customer view and we want to toggle between a read-only view and an edit view of the customer information. Let's look at how we would do this. Upon completing this chapter, you will have a good understanding of how compose works in Aurelia and when and where you would want to consider using it.

When Not to Use Compose

For most cases, consider using custom elements when you want to use reusable components in Aurelia. You get several benefits by using custom elements over compose. Your custom elements are fully encapsulated and are easier to maintain and understand. Custom elements adhere to strict guidelines when interacting with the component from the outside by using @bindable properties. Custom elements can be made global so that you can reference them from any view without any other knowledge where it came from.

If you know that the markup for your view is going to be static and does not need to change, try to use custom elements first before considering compose.

When to Use Compose

Now that we know when not to use compose, there are times when a dynamic view comes in really handy for building a great user experience. Let's use the example provided at the beginning of the chapter and see how we can satisfy this requirement.

179

© Matthew Duffield 2018
M. Duffield, *Practical App Development with Aurelia*, https://doi.org/10.1007/978-1-4842-3402-0_17

We are interested in creating a customer screen that has a read-only and editable view. This is where compose can really shine as well as mitigate redundancies. If we would have created two separate custom elements for each of the views, we would most likely have a lot of redundancies between the view models of each. However, with compose, it is possible to have multiple views bound to the same view model. This is what we are going to do now. Figure 17-1 shows our customer read-only view.

Toggle View

Customer View

First Name: John

Last Name: Doe

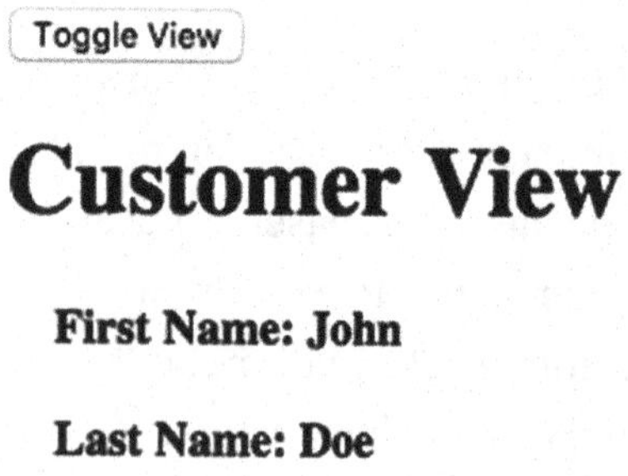

Figure 17-1. *Customer read-only view*

If we now click the Toggle View button, we will see Figure 17-2.

Toggle View

Customer Edit

First Name

John

Last Name

Doe

Figure 17-2. *Customer edit view*

As you can see, we are simply representing the data with different views. You will also see that we are using the same view model for both views.

Let's look at the code we used to accomplish this. Consider the app.html file:

```
<template>
  <button click.delegate="toggleView()">
    Toggle View
  </button>
  <compose view.bind="currentView"
    view model="./resources/customer">
    </compose>
</template>
```

The app.html file has two elements, a button and a compose element. The button is used to toggle our views and the compose is used to bind our views as well as define the view model.

Let's now look at how the app.js file is set up:

```
export class App {

  customerView = './resources/customer-view.html';
  customerEdit = './resources/customer-edit.html';

  constructor() {
    this.currentView = this.customerView;
  }

  toggleView() {
    if (this.currentView === this.customerView) {
      this.currentView = this.customerEdit;
    } else {
      this.currentView = this.customerView;
    }
  }
}
```

We see that we have two properties that provide the location of each view. We are initializing the app.js view model to set the view to read-only view in the constructor. In the toggleView function, we swap the currentView between the customerEdit or customerView properties.

This simple logic could be extended to handle a wizard of multiple views while only using a single view model.

Now let's look at our customer.js view model code:

```
export class Customer {

  firstName = "John";
  lastName = "Doe";

  constructor() {
  }
}
```

This view model simply encapsulates the data for which our views will be bound. Let's see what the customer-view.html file look like:

```
<template>
  <require from="./customer.css"></require>

  <h1>Customer View</h1>
  <form class="customer">
    <fieldset>
      <label>First Name: ${firstName}</label>
    </fieldset>
    <fieldset>
      <label>Last Name: ${lastName}</label>
    </fieldset>
  </form>
</template>
```

We are including a customer.css file just to help with the overall look of the view. Next you will see that we have an H1 describing the view. We have a form with a couple of fieldsets that display our data from the view model.

Let's now look at the customer-edit.html file:

```
<template>
  <require from="./customer.css"></require>
  <h1>Customer Edit</h1>
  <form class="customer">
    <fieldset>
      <label>First Name</label>
```

```
    <input value.bind="firstName">
  </fieldset>
  <fieldset>
    <label>Last Name</label>
    <input value.bind="lastName">
  </fieldset>
  </form>
</template>
```

Again, we see a lot of similarities with some slight changes. Having two views can come in handy if you decide that the overall look and feel between read-only and edit views should be significantly different. If you were to do this in a single file, it could get messy and make it harder to manage and support.

For consistency, let's look at what was included in the customer.css file:

```
form.customer fieldset {
  border-color: transparent;
}
form.customer label {
  font-weight: bold;
}
form.customer input {
  width: 100%;
  margin-top: 5px;
}
```

Again, a lot of this markup could go away if we were to use a third-party CSS library like Twitter Bootstrap or something else.

Summary

You now have a good understanding of using the compose element in Aurelia. Take care when using this element over creating custom elements, but don't be afraid to roll up your sleeves and create some dynamic screens that respond to some form of criteria. Compose is provided to make your development easier and to satisfy the times when you wish the framework could do just a little more or be a little more flexible. This is one of those such gems.

Dynamic Views

We have seen where the compose custom element comes in handy, but there may be scenarios where it would be really nice to serve dynamic views. In this chapter, we will look into how Aurelia has this type of flexibility out of the box. When you have finished this chapter, you should have a firm understanding of how you can employ each of the techniques and when you would want to use them. Let's get started.

getViewStrategy

We have already covered the view life cycle, but one thing that we left out is the function getViewStrategy. Every view model has the ability to opt-in and utilize the getViewStrategy function. This gives us the ability to dictate how we want our views to be loaded. By convention, Aurelia looks for views that have the same name as the view model. We can completely override this. Aurelia also provides some helpers to make this easier. Perhaps you would like to load a string representation of your view? This is extremely easy with the InlineViewStrategy. Consider the following page1.js file:

```
import {InlineViewStrategy} from 'aurelia-templating';

export class Page1 {

  getViewStrategy() {
    let template = `
    <template>
      <section>
        <h2>Dynamic View!</h2>
      </section>
    </template>
    `;
```

```
    let vs = new InlineViewStrategy(template, this);
    return vs;
  }
}
```

As you can see from the preceding, there is not a lot of ceremony involved with providing your own views for a given view model. We are importing the InlineViewStrategy and returning a new instance of it passing in our template and a reference to this instance so that it has the correct binding context.

Figure 18-1 shows what the view looks like.

Dynamic Views   Page 1   Page 2

Dynamic View!

Figure 18-1. Page1.js

Let's take this a step further and make the view we create more dynamic. Consider the following page2.js file:

```
import {InlineViewStrategy} from 'aurelia-templating';
import {HttpClient} from 'aurelia-fetch-client';

export class Page2 {
  static inject = [HttpClient];

  users = [];
  view = '';

  constructor(http) {
    this.http = http;
    this.baseUrl = `https://randomuser.me/`;
    this.http.configure(config => {
      config
```

```
        .useStandardConfiguration()
        .withBaseUrl(this.baseUrl);
    });
  }

  activate() {
    return this.getUsers().then(data => {
      this.users = data.results;
      this.view = `
<template>
  <div class="users">
    <div class="user" repeat.for="user of users">
      <img src.bind="user.picture.medium">
      <span class="">\${user.name.first} \${user.name.last}
      </span>
    </div>
  </div>
</template>`;
    });
  }

  getViewStrategy() {
    let vs = new InlineViewStrategy(this.view, this);
    return vs;
  }

  getUsers(numberUsers = 6) {
    let path = `api?nat=us&results=${numberUsers}`;
    return this.http.fetch(path)
      .then(response => response.json());
  }
}
```

Just like the preview view model, we are bringing in the InlineViewStrategy. We also are bringing in HttpClient using the aurelia-fetch-client. We inject the HttpClient into our constructor and configure the instance.

Now that we know that our view won't render until the 'activate' function has returned from its Promise, we are calling a helper function that returns a Promise that returns some random users. When the Promise returns, we set a local 'users' array as well as construct a view to be used with our getViewStrategy function. Because the view constructed is simply an ECMAScript 2015 Template literal, we need to escape the '$' character so that it does not try to evaluate the expression until rendered. Everything else is exactly the same.

Figure 18-2 is a screenshot of page2.js rendered.

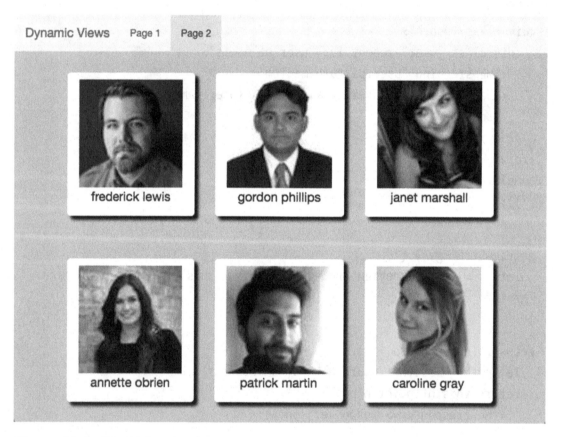

Figure 18-2. *Page2.js*

Take a moment and reflect on how we are rendering our view. It would not be a stretch of the imagination to have the view stored in a database. This would allow you to simply modify your views without ever needing to redeploy your application. Albeit you would want to have some form of caching of your views fetched, it is not unreasonable to have such an infrastructure in place if so desired.

Enhance

We have seen just how powerful 'getViewStrategy' is and how we can use it in our applications. Let's now look at another approach to making our view dynamic. Consider a scenario in which you would like to have dynamic HTML injected into your view that contains bindings. You would also like to be able to modify this HTML somehow and still have the bindings work. This is where the 'enhance' function from the 'aurelia-templating-engine' shines. Let's begin by looking at the rendered view (Figure 18-3).

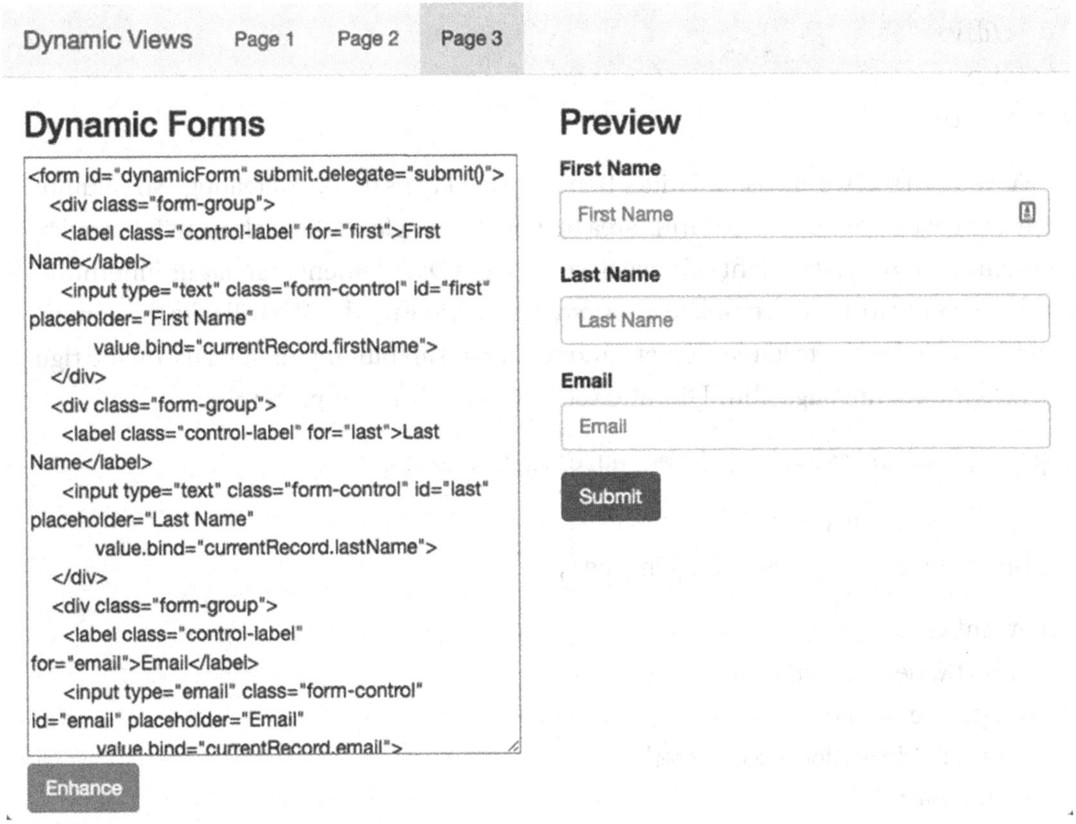

Figure 18-3. *Page 3 before enhance*

189

We will use the left side of the view to construct the right side. Consider the following page3.html file:

```
<template>
  <div class="dynamic-form">
    <div class="col-sm-6">
      <h3>Dynamic Forms</h3>
      <textarea value.bind="viewTemplate">
      </textarea>
      <button class="btn btn-success"
        click.delegate="update()">Enhance</button>
    </div>
    <div class="col-sm-6">
      <h3>Preview</h1>
      <div id="dynamicHost" innerhtml.bind="viewTemplate">
      </div>
    </div>
  </div>
</template>
```

As you can see, we are using Twitter Bootstrap to help us out with creating two columns. On the left, we have a dynamic forms area that hosts a single textarea element followed by a button element. On the right side, we have a simple DIV element that has its innerhtml attribute bound to a 'viewTemplate' property on our view model. We will take the content that is provided in the textarea element and render it with bindings in the DIV on the right.

Let's look at the page3.html file and see how we can accomplish this:

```
import {TemplatingEngine} from 'aurelia-framework';

export class Page3 {
  static inject = [TemplatingEngine];

  currentRecord = {
    firstName: 'John',
    lastName: 'Doe',
    email: 'john.doe@email.com',
    isActive: true
  };
```

```
  viewTemplate = `
  <form id="dynamicForm" submit.delegate="submit()">
    <div class="form-group">
      <label class="control-label" for="first">First Name</label>
      <input type="text" class="form-control" id="first" placeholder="First Name"
             value.bind="currentRecord.firstName">
    </div>
    <div class="form-group">
      <label class="control-label" for="last">Last Name</label>
      <input type="text" class="form-control" id="last" placeholder="Last Name"
             value.bind="currentRecord.lastName">
    </div>
    <div class="form-group">
      <label class="control-label" for="email">Email</label>
      <input type="email" class="form-control" id="email" placeholder="Email"
             value.bind="currentRecord.email">
    </div>
    <button type="submit" class="btn btn-primary">Submit</button>
  </form>
  `.trim();

  constructor(templatingEngine) {
    this.templatingEngine = templatingEngine;
  }

  update() {
    const selector = '#dynamicForm';
    const el = document.querySelector(selector);
    if (el) {
      this.templatingEngine.enhance({element: el, bindingContext: this });
    }
  }

  submit() {
    console.log('submitting...', this.currentRecord);
  }
}
```

The majority of this file really has to do with the dynamic HTML that we want to have rendered. We start by importing the TemplatingEngine from the 'aurelia-framework' and injecting it into our constructor. Next, we set up some class properties that we will use in the view. We have a currentRecord property, which is what our dynamic form will ultimately bind to. Then, we have a viewTemplate property, which is what our textarea is bound to and which allows us to make changes for testing our markup. We have an 'update' function that will allow us to enhance our view. It is this function that does all the work of enhancing an element along with a binding context. We achieve this by finding the ID of the form element and then simply calling the enhance function providing the element as well as a reference to 'this', which represents our view model. We want the enhanced element to be able to access the currentRecord as well as the 'submit' function.

Let's actually enhance our view by calling the 'update' function. Figure 18-4 shows what our screen now looks like after enhancing the view:

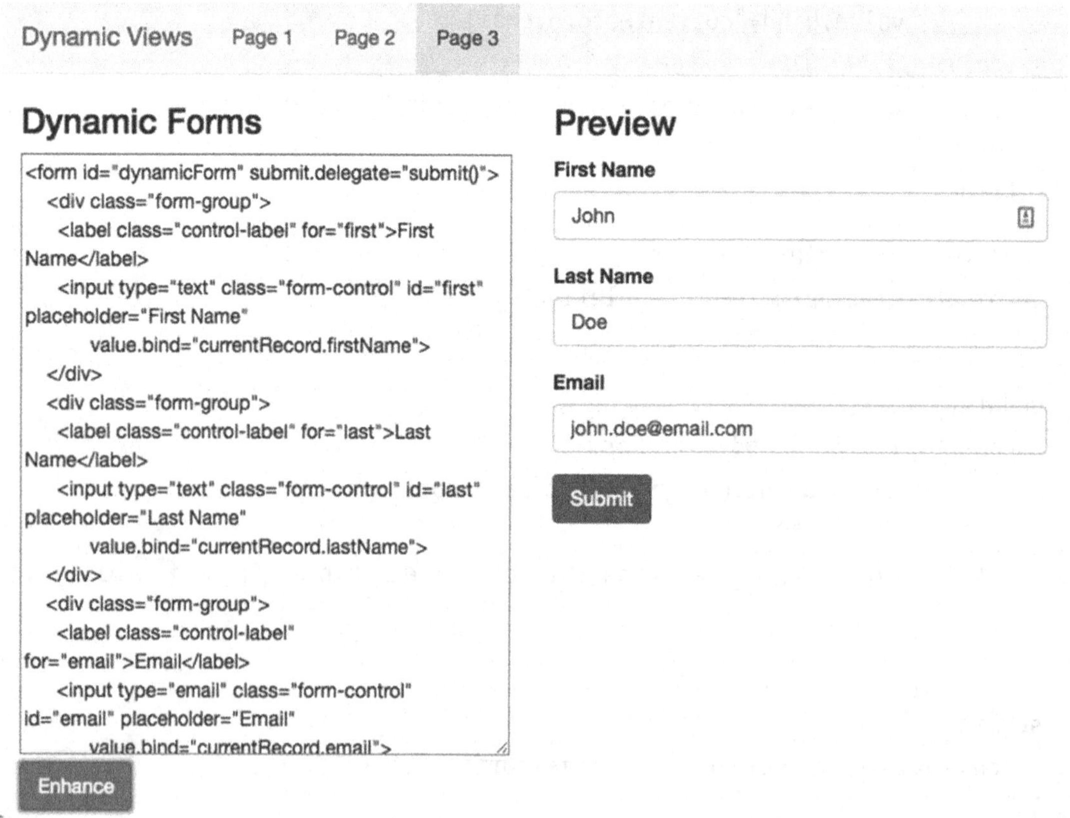

Figure 18-4. *Page 3 after enhance*

As you can see, our bindings are now working. If we clicked the Submit button, we would see Figure 18-5.

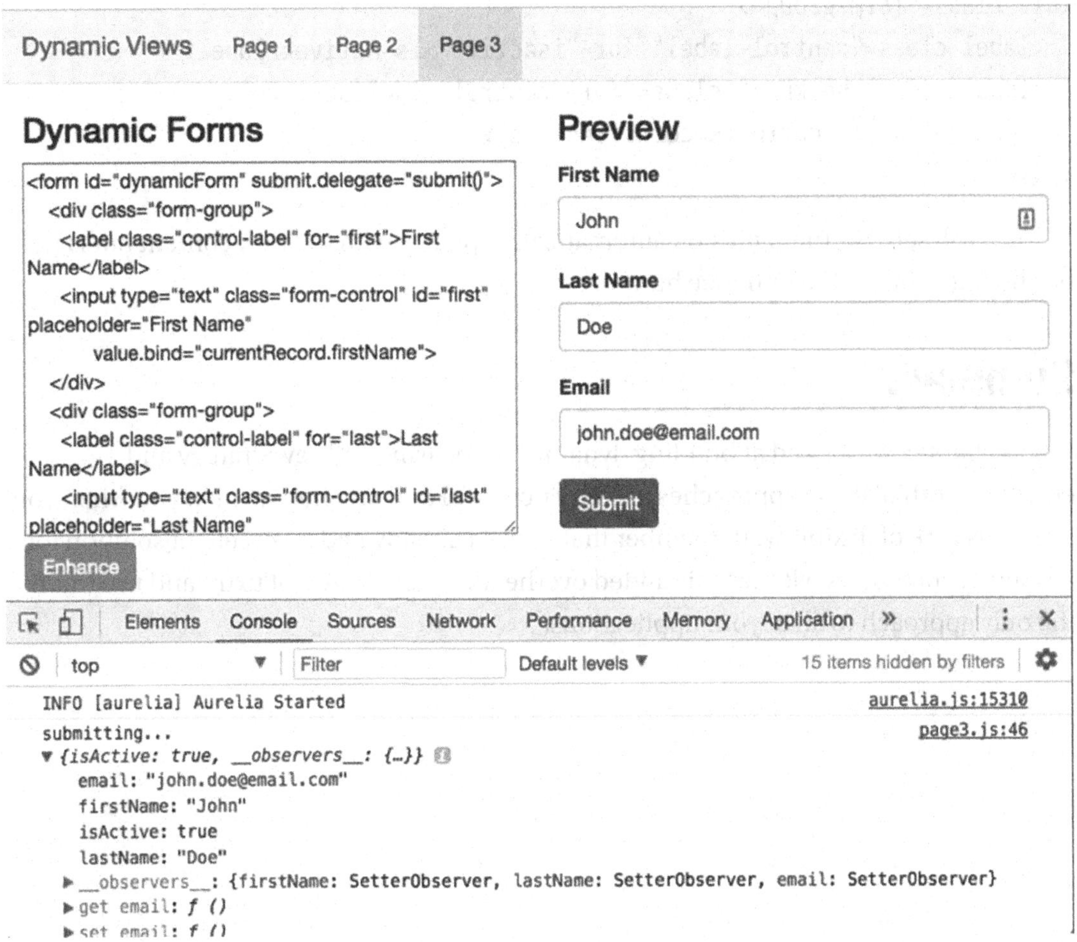

Figure 18-5. *Page 3 after submit*

As you can see, the ability to enhance an element is extremely powerful. Although it may not be needed for every scenario while building your applications, it is very nice to know that you have this kind of flexibility.

Take a moment and play with the textarea element on the left. You could add a check box like the following:

```
<div class="form-group">
  <label class="control-label" for="isactive">Is Active</label>
  <input type="checkbox" class="form-control" id="isactive"
    checked.bind="currentRecord.isActive">
</div>
```

You will see that the right side automatically updates with the new content but is not bound until you hit the Enhance button.

Summary

In this chapter, we looked at building dynamic views using getViewStrategy and enhance. Both of these approaches are very powerful and are there to help you when you need this type of flexibility. Remember that Aurelia already had an excellent solution for rendering your views without this added overhead. So take care not to try and use this as the only approach to all of your applications.

CHAPTER 19

Creating Features

We now know how to write custom elements and attributes. It is pretty easy to create reusable components and reference them from any view by simply using the "require" tag in your HTML. We are going to learn how to reference our own components globally and remove the need for the "require" tag. Upon completing this chapter, you should have a firm understanding of how to define features in your code. You will be able to register your feature as well as gain access to all of your components from your HTML without using the "require" tag.

What Are Features?

We use features in our applications to allow us to organize components that can be naturally grouped together. If you follow the project structure generated by the Aurelia CLI, you will more than likely have something that looks like the following:

```
Project name/
  src/
    resources/
      attributes/
        circle/
          circle.js
        input-mask/
          input-mask.js
        set-focus/
          set-focus.js
      binding-behaviors/
        stop-propagation-binding-behavior.js
      elements/
```

© Matthew Duffield 2018
M. Duffield, *Practical App Development with Aurelia*, https://doi.org/10.1007/978-1-4842-3402-0_19

```
listview/
  listview-item.html
  listview-item.js
  listview.css
  listview.html
  listview.js
multi-selector/
  multi-selector-item.html
  multi-selector-item.js
  multi-selector.css
  multi-selector.html
  multi-selector.js
nav-bar/
  nav-bar.html
tab-control/
  tab-control.css
  tab-control.html
  tab-control.js
  tab-item.html
  tab-item.js
value-converters/
  date-format-value-converter.js
  sort-value-converter.js
  time-ago-value-converter.js
index.js
```

In the preceding structure, we are only looking at the "resources" folder. You may have other folders in your application structure. We are going to assume that the "resources" folder is what we want to use for our feature definition.

Configuring Global Resources

You may have noticed that we have a single file off of the "resources" folder, index.js. It is this file that allows us to configure our feature globally. This file must export a single function, "configure". Inside the function, we will use the "config" parameter to configure our global resources as shown in the following:

```
export function configure(config) {
  config.globalResources([
    './attributes/circle/circle'
    './attributes/input-mask/input-mask',
    './attributes/set-focus/set-focus',
    './elements/listview/listview',
    './elements/listview/listview-item',
    './elements/multi-selector/multi-selector',
    './elements/tab-control/tab-control',
    './elements/tab-control/tab-item',
  ]);
}
```

Once we have listed out all of the components we wish to make global, we can save the file.

Next, we need to register our feature with Aurelia so that it knows about our components. We do this in the "main.js" file:

```
export function configure(aurelia) {
  aurelia.use
    .standardConfiguration()
    .developmentLogging()
    .feature('resources');

  aurelia.start().then(a => a.setRoot());
}
```

As you can see from the preceding, it is pretty straightforward to include our feature in our application and have global access to our components in our views. In this example, Aurelia looks for a folder with the name "resources" and then expects there to be an "index.js" file within the folder.

If we follow this convention, it is easy to see that we could have named our "resources" folder anything as long as we had an "index.js" file inside that managed the globalResources array.

Markup Scenario

If we hadn't included our "resources" in our "main.js" file, an example using the
"set-focus" custom attribute would look like the following:

```
<template>
  <require from="../resources/attributes/set-focus/set-focus"></require>

  <form>
    <div class="form-group">
      <label for="name">
        Name
      </label>
      <input id="name"
        type="text"
        value.bind="currentRecord.name"
        set-focus>
    </div>
  </form>
</template>
```

However, if we do include the "feature" in our "main.js" file, then our code would
look like the following:

```
<template>
  <form>
    <div class="form-group">
      <label for="name">
        Name
      </label>
      <input id="name"
        type="text"
        value.bind="currentRecord.name"
        set-focus>
    </div>
  </form>
</template>
```

You may think that this is not that big of a deal, but if you are bringing in a lot of custom elements, custom attributes, and so forth, you could have a substantial list of "require" tags at the top of your markup.

Summary

Features are a great technique for keeping our code clean and providing a means for grouping and categorizing your components. You will find that you will appreciate the time savings and the structure that features provide you while developing your applications. We have looked at the simple steps required to make your custom attributes, custom elements, and so forth globally available as resources. Don't be afraid to create multiple "features" and register them in your "main.js" file.

CHAPTER 20

Creating Plug-ins

In the last chapter, we learned how to create features that we could in turn use in our applications. In this chapter, we are going to learn how we can take our features a step further and create plug-ins so that we can install them via the CLI or Node Package Manager (NPM). We will look at creating a Node Package of your source code that will best structure your plug-in.

Going from a Feature to a Plug-in

Just as with features, it is important to structure your plug-ins in a way that is consistent with most of the official Aurelia plug-ins. Let's take a look at the file structure a majority of Aurelia plug-ins use:

```
build/
dist/
doc/
src/
test/
```

You may want to create this base structure and put placeholder files in it so that you can have it as a starting repository. This way you use the structure for any new plug-in you wish to work on. One of the easiest ways to ensure that your plug-in is working is to use an existing Aurelia CLI project. In this project, create a bundle that only contains your plug-in and then copy this file to another project and configure the project to use it. Let's use the input-mask as an example and see if we can get this working.

© Matthew Duffield 2018
M. Duffield, *Practical App Development with Aurelia*, https://doi.org/10.1007/978-1-4842-3402-0_20

Existing Aurelia CLI Project

In this project, we will configure the CLI to create a bundle for the input-mask custom attribute. In the aurelia.json file under the aurelia_project folder, make sure the following is the first entry for the bundles array:

```
{
  "name": "index.js",
  "source": [
    "**/resources/index.js"
  ]
},
```

If this is not the first entry, the target file will be empty when you try to create the bundle. We are basically telling the CLI to take everything from our resources folder and bundle it up as a separate item. Here is the output from generating the index.js bundle:

```
define('resources/index',['exports'], function (exports) {
  'use strict';

  Object.defineProperty(exports, "__esModule", {
    value: true
  });
  exports.configure = configure;
  function configure(config) {
    config.globalResources(['./attributes/input-mask/input-mask']);
  }
});
//# sourceMappingURL=index.js.map
```

We need to do a little work in order to use this generated file. The main reason for this is the fact that we have chosen to leave our source files in the exact same location as when we were using them. We need them now to be flattened out, and this means that we can remove all of the relative paths except the actual files. The following is the same file with the updated changes. We removed the 'resources/index' entry in the define function as well as the '/attributes/input-mask' from the globalResources function. We also removed the sourceMapping entry but that is more of a preference:

```
define(['exports'], function (exports) {
  'use strict';

  Object.defineProperty(exports, "__esModule", {
    value: true
  });
  exports.configure = configure;
  function configure(config) {
    config.globalResources(['./input-mask']);
  }
});
```

We have completed creating our index.js file; let's now create our input-mask.js bundle. Add the following entry right after the index.js bundle:

```
{
  "name": "input-mask.js",
  "source": [
    "[**/resources/attributes/input-mask/*.js]",
    "**/resources/attributes/input-mask/*.{css,html}"
  ]
},
```

This simply is creating a new input-mask.js bundle targeting the input-mask folder under the attributes folder. The following is the output from generating this file:

```
define('resources/attributes/input-mask/input-mask',['exports', 'aurelia-
framework', 'aurelia-pal'], function (exports, _aureliaFramework, _aureliaPal) {
  'use strict';

  Object.defineProperty(exports, "__esModule", {
    value: true
  });
  exports.InputMask = undefined;

  function _initDefineProp(target, property, descriptor, context) {
    if (!descriptor) return;
    Object.defineProperty(target, property, {
      enumerable: descriptor.enumerable,
```

```
    configurable: descriptor.configurable,
    writable: descriptor.writable,
    value: descriptor.initializer ? descriptor.initializer.call(context) : void 0
  });
}

function _classCallCheck(instance, Constructor) {
  if (!(instance instanceof Constructor)) {
    throw new TypeError("Cannot call a class as a function");
  }
}

function _applyDecoratedDescriptor(target, property, decorators,
descriptor, context) {
  var desc = {};
  Object['ke' + 'ys'](descriptor).forEach(function (key) {
    desc[key] = descriptor[key];
  });
  desc.enumerable = !!desc.enumerable;
  desc.configurable = !!desc.configurable;

  if ('value' in desc || desc.initializer) {
    desc.writable = true;
  }

  desc = decorators.slice().reverse().reduce(function (desc, decorator) {
    return decorator(target, property, desc) || desc;
  }, desc);

  if (context && desc.initializer !== void 0) {
    desc.value = desc.initializer ? desc.initializer.call(context) : void 0;
    desc.initializer = undefined;
  }

  if (desc.initializer === void 0) {
    Object['define' + 'Property'](target, property, desc);
    desc = null;
  }
```

```
  return desc;
}

function _initializerWarningHelper(descriptor, context) {
  throw new Error('Decorating class property failed. Please ensure that
  transform-class-properties is enabled.');
}

var _dec, _class, _desc, _value, _class2, _descriptor, _class3, _temp;

var InputMask = exports.InputMask = (_dec = (0, _aureliaFramework.
customAttribute)('input-mask'), _dec(_class = (_class2 =
(_temp = _class3 = function () {
  function InputMask(element) {
    _classCallCheck(this, InputMask);

    _initDefineProp(this, 'pattern', _descriptor, this);

    this.element = element;
    if (element instanceof HTMLInputElement) {
      this.element = element;
    } else {
      throw new Error('The input-mask attribute can only be applied on
      Input elements.');
    }
  }

  InputMask.prototype.attached = function attached() {
    this.element.addEventListener("keydown", this.keyDownHandler.bind(this));
  };

  InputMask.prototype.detached = function detached() {
    this.element.removeEventListener("keydown", this.keyDownHandler.
    bind(this));
  };

  InputMask.prototype.keyDownHandler = function keyDownHandler(e) {
    var value = e.target.value;
```

205

```
      var isInt = Number.isInteger(Number.parseInt(e.key));
      var key = e.key.toLowerCase();
      var valueLen = value.length;
      var patternLen = this.pattern.length;
      var char = this.pattern[valueLen];
      var options = {
        e: e,
        value: value,
        isInt: isInt,
        key: key,
        valueLen: valueLen,
        patternLen: patternLen,
        char: char
      };
      var result = true;
      if (this.isValidNonInputKey(key)) {} else if (valueLen === patternLen) {
        e.preventDefault();
        result = false;
      } else if (char === '#' && isInt) {} else if (this.processKey(options))
      {} else {
        e.preventDefault();
        result = false;
      }
      return result;
    };

    InputMask.prototype.processKey = function processKey(options) {
      var key = options.key,
          char = options.char,
          isInt = options.isInt,
          valueLen = options.valueLen,
          e = options.e;
```

```
    if (key === char) {
      return true;
    } else if (char !== '#' && isInt) {
      var nextChar = this.pattern[valueLen + 1];
      if (nextChar === ' ') {
        e.target.value = e.target.value + char + ' ';
      } else {
        e.target.value = e.target.value + char;
      }
      return true;
    }
    return false;
  };

  InputMask.prototype.isValidNonInputKey = function isValidNonInputKey(key) {
    var keys = ["backspace", "arrowleft", "arrowright", "arrowup",
    "arrowdown", "home", "end", "tab"];
    return keys.includes(key);
  };

  return InputMask;
}(), _class3.inject = [_aureliaPal.DOM.Element], _temp), (_descriptor =
_applyDecoratedDescriptor(_class2.prototype, 'pattern', [_aureliaFramework.
bindable], {
  enumerable: true,
  initializer: function initializer() {
    return '';
  }
})), _class2)) || _class);
});
//# sourceMappingURL=input-mask.js.map
```

The only change necessary for this file is the very first line. Again, we want to remove the relative path, 'resources/attributes/input-mask/input-mask'. We also will remove the very last line referencing the sourceMapping.

You now have your index.js and input-mask.js files created. These two files can go in the dist/amd/ folder. By default the Aurelia CLI generates modules in the AMD format. This can also be changed if you go to the aurelia.json file and refer to the 'transpiler' section as shown in the following:

```
"transpiler": {
  "id": "babel",
  "displayName": "Babel",
  "fileExtension": ".js",
  "options": {
    "plugins": [
      "transform-es2015-modules-amd"
    ]
  },
  "source": "src/**/*.js"
},
```

When you create an Aurelia CLI project targeting Babel, you will have the 'transform-es2015-modules-amd' and 'transform-es2015-modules-commonjs' plug-ins available out of the box. You can simply change out which target you wish to use for creating the other formats. You can also put your tests and documentation in the corresponding folders of your structure so that they are part of the repository when you commit.

This was a very contrived and painful approach to creating the bundled file formats for a given plug-in. Luckily, there exists an aurelia-plugin repository whose sole task is to make it easier to create plug-ins for Aurelia. You can find the plug-in here: https://github.com/aurelia/skeleton-plugin

Also, the Aurelia team is actively working on making it easier to produce plug-ins directly from the CLI.

Publishing your Plug-in

Now that we have our plug-in coded and our bundles generated appropriately, we need to make it available for consumption by other developers. The most common approach to this is to have your project source controlled with something like GitHub and then use NPM to publish it. NPM makes extensive use of your package.json file, so it is important that it is accurate. Take some time to ensure that you have all key properties filled out.

Execute the following command to publish your project:

```
npm publish ./
```

If this is the first time you have published to NPM on your development machine, you may also need to provide credentials as follows:

```
npm set init.author.name "Your name"
npm set init.author.email your@email.com
npm set init.author.url http://yourblob.com
npm adduser
```

These steps will get you set up for publishing to NPM.

After you have published and have made modifications to your code base and committed those changes to GitHub, it is important that you increment the version number in the package.json file prior to publishing the update.

Using Your Plug-in

You are finally ready to use your plug-in just like all the rest of the plug-ins available. Let's say that you created your plug-in with the name 'input-mask'; then you could execute the following command:

```
au install input-mask
```

or

```
npm install –save input-mask
```

Next, you will need to configure your main.js file to include the installed plug-in as follows:

```
import {PLATFORM} from 'aurelia-pal';

export function configure(aurelia) {
  aurelia.use
    .standardConfiguration()
    .developmentLogging()
    .plugin(PLATFORM.moduleName('input-mask'));

  aurelia.start().then(a => a.setRoot());
}
```

You only need to use the input-mask plug-in in your code like the following:

```
<template>
  <form>
    <div class="form-group">
      <label for="phone">
        Phone Number
      </label>
      <input id="phone"
        type="text"
        value.bind="currentRecord.phone"
        input-mask="pattern: (###) ###-####;"
        placeholder="(555) 555-1234">
    </div>
  </form>
</template>
```

That's it! You now have your custom attribute available as a plug-in for use by any developer.

Summary

Plug-ins are very powerful in that they let you bundle up functionalities and deliver them as NPM packages. This is one area where it is still a little complex, but the Aurelia team working hard on making this a seamless activity via the Aurelia CLI. Take your time and play with plug-ins. It is okay if you don't get them working on the first attempt. You will find it rewarding once you have everything working and you can start sharing your plug-ins with the rest of the community.

CHAPTER 21

Animations

Although animations might not be part of your core requirements when building an application, they often add some polish and convey a feeling of comfort and acceptance to the end user. We are going to be looking at animations and the aurelia-animator-css plug-in. This plug-in allows you to use CSS to configure and control how our animations behave. By the time you complete this chapter, you will have a good command of using the aurelia-animator-css plug-in in your own applications.

Animation Plug-ins

We will be covering the aurelia-animator-css plug-in, but there are other plug-ins that you may be interested in that provide similar if not more advanced capabilities:

- aurelia-animator-css - `https://github.com/aurelia/animator-css`

- aurelia-animator-greensock - `https://gooy.github.io/aurelia-animator-greensock/`

- aurelia-animator-velocity - `http://gooy.github.io/aurelia-animator-velocity/`

Take a second and look at each of these plug-ins.

Aurelia-Animator-CSS Plug-in

Let's take a look at what it takes to use the aurelia-animator-css plug-in in our own application. We are going to first start by animating our router. This is probably one of the most common scenarios that you will want to support.

211

© Matthew Duffield 2018
M. Duffield, *Practical App Development with Aurelia*, https://doi.org/10.1007/978-1-4842-3402-0_21

CSS3 Animations

The aurelia-animator-css plug-in relies on CSS3 animations. The plug-in relies on a simple convention when it comes to providing CSS classes. In order to use the plug-in, you must provide the 'au-animate' class on the element of your choice. There are several classes that Aurelia manages once you have identified the element with the 'au-animate' class:

- au-enter

- au-enter-active

- au-leave

- au-leave-active

We can provide whatever CSS rules we want for each of these classes.

Animations and Routes

It is possible to have animations when your routes change. When you navigate from one route to another, the old view is swapped out for the new view. Table 21-1 lists out the possible strategies to add the 'swap-order' attribute to the 'router-view' custom element.

Table 21-1. *Adding the swap-order Attribute to the router-view Custom Element*

Name	Description
before	This will animate the new view prior to removing the old view
with	This will animate the new and old views at the same time
after	This will animate the new view after the old view has been removed (Default)

It is also possible to bind to the 'swap-order' attribute. This gives you the flexibility of changing the animation behavior dynamically if you want.

Let's move on and look at what it takes to get animations working.

Getting Our Animations Set Up

We first are going to need to install the plug-in. You can do this by using the Aurelia CLI and executing the following command:

```
au install aurelia-animator-css
```

Or if you want to use NPM:

```
npm install aurelia-animator-css --save
```

Once we have the plug-in installed, we are going to need to make sure that Aurelia is aware and loads the plug-in. We do this by modifying the main.js file:

```
export function configure(aurelia) {
  aurelia.use
    .standardConfiguration()
    .developmentLogging();

  aurelia.use.plugin('aurelia-animator-css');

  aurelia.start().then(a => a.setRoot());
}
```

As you can see from the preceding, we have come across most of this already before. What is new here is that we are registering a plug-in, 'aurelia-animator-css'. This will load the plug-in and make it available for us to use within our application.

Now, we need to update our router so that it will animate when routes change. We will do this by modifying our app.html file:

```
<template>
  <require from="./app.css"></require>
  <require from="./nav-bar.html"></require>

  <nav-bar router.bind="router"></nav-bar>

  <div class="page-host" view-spy="">
    <router-view></router-view>
  </div>
</template>
```

In this first example we are not even providing the 'swap-order' custom attribute. Let's define some views so that we can transition between them. The following is page1.html:

```
<template>
  <section class="au-animate page1">
    <h1>Page 1</h1>
  </section>
</template>
```

Take note that we are introducing a class, 'au-animate'. This tells Aurelia that we want to animate this element. Here is the view model, page1.js:

```
export class Page1 {

  constructor() {  }
}
```

As you can see, this is extremely simple but we are more concerned with the animation than the implementation details of our view and view model. Let's create one more view, page2.html:

```
<template>
  <section class="au-animate page2">
    <h1>Page 2</h1>
  </section>
</template>
```

Here is the view model, page2.js:

```
export class Page2 {

  constructor() {  }
}
```

Let's now look at our router definition in the app.js file:

```
export class App {

  configureRouter(config, router) {
    config.title = 'Animations';
    config.map([
      {route: ["", "page1"], moduleId: "src/page1", href: "#/page1", title:
      "Page 1", nav: true},
      {route: "page2", moduleId: "src/page2", href: "#/page2", title:
      "Page 2", nav: true},
    ]);

    this.router = router;
  }
}
```

Notice that our routes do not require any changes.

Now, let's shift gears and focus on the CSS that is required to get our animation working. Take a look at the followingapp.css file:

```
.user-select-none { user-select: none; }
.page-host {
  position: absolute;
  left: 0;
  right: 0;
  top: 50px;
  bottom: 0;
  overflow-x: hidden;
  overflow-y: auto;
}
section.au-animate {
  padding: 20px;
  position: absolute;
  width: 100%;
  height: 100%;
}
```

```
.page1 {
  background-color: lightskyblue;
}
.page2 {
  background-color: limegreen;
}
/* Slide Left Animation */
section.au-enter-active {
  animation: slideInLeft 1s;
}
section.au-leave-active {
  animation: slideOutLeft 1s;
}
/* CSS3 Animations */
@keyframes slideInLeft {
  0% { transform: translate3d(100%, 0, 0); }
  100% { transform: none; }
}
@keyframes slideOutLeft {
  0% { transform: none; }
  100% { transform: translate3d(-100%, 0, 0); }
}
```

Here, we are targeting the 'au-enter-active' and 'au-leave-active' classes to perform our animation. What this animation does is slide the existing view from right to left. At the same time, it slides the new view from right to left. You can see that we created different background colors for each view so that you could see the animation more clearly.

Notice that our animation definition for both the 'au-enter-active' and 'au-leave-active' animations have been set to take one second. You can play with this as well and tune it to what seems natural and smooth for your applications.

Figure 21-1 shows a screenshot of what your application should look like after page1 has been navigated.

Figure 21-1. *Slide animation*

Let's see what else we can do with our CSS animations.

Adding/Removing Items

Let's extend our application by adding another page, 'page3'. This page will behave exactly as the other two pages but will also have a simple list that we can add and remove items. We will want to fade in newly added items to the list and fade out items removed from the list.

Here is the page3.html file:

```
<template>
  <section class="au-animate page3">
    <h1>Page 3</h1>

    <h3>Grocery List
      <button class="btn btn-primary"
        click.delegate="addToList()">Add New Item</button>
    </h3>
    <ul>
      <li repeat.for="item of items">${item}</li>
    </ul>
  </section>
</template>
```

Let's now look at the page3.js file:

```
import {bindable} from 'aurelia-framework';

export class Page3 {

  @bindable items = [
    'apples',
    'cereal'
  ];

  constructor() {

  }

  addToList() {
    let item = "donuts";
    this.items.push(item);
  }

}
```

Our view model is now set up to handle adding new items. For now, we are simply adding 'donuts' to our grocery list.

As a reminder, here is how we get our page3 added to our routes in the app.js file:

```
import 'jQuery';
import 'bootstrap';

export class App {

  configureRouter(config, router) {
    config.title = 'Animations';
    config.map([
      {route: ["", "page1"], moduleId: "src/page1", href: "#/page1", title:
      "Page 1", nav: true},
      {route: "page2", moduleId: "src/page2", href: "#/page2", title:
      "Page 2", nav: true},
      {route: "page3", moduleId: "src/page3", href: "#/page3", title:
      "Page 3", nav: true},
    ]);
```

```
    this.router = router;
  }

}
```

Now, let's modify our page3.html and app.css files to support animating adding items to the list. We will start with page3.html:

```
<template>
  <section class="au-animate page3">
    <h1>Page 3</h1>

    <h3>Grocery List
      <button class="btn btn-primary"
      click.delegate="addToList()">Add New Item</button>
    </h3>
    <ul class="list-animation">
      <li repeat.for="item of items"
        class="au-animate">
        <i class="fa fa-trash" click.delegate="removeFromList($index)"></i>
        ${item}
      </li>
    </ul>
  </section>
</template>
```

The markup is pretty much the same with the exception of the UL element and contents. We added a "list-animation" class to the UL for styling. On the LI element, we added the necessary class "au-animate". We also added an I element so that we could click the trash icon to remove an item. Let's look at what we had to do in our view model, page3.js:

```
import {bindable} from 'aurelia-framework';

export class Page3 {

  @bindable items = [
    'apples',
    'cereal'
  ];
```

```
  constructor() {

  }

  addToList() {
    let item = "donuts";
    this.items.push(item);
  }
  removeFromList(index) {
    this.items.splice(index, 1);
  }

}
```

The only difference here is the addition of the "removeFromList" function. In this function, we simply splice a single item off of the array. Finally, let's look at what we needed to add to the app.css file to get the animations to work for adding and removing items:

```
.user-select-none { user-select: none; }
.page-host {
  position: absolute;
  left: 0;
  right: 0;
  top: 50px;
  bottom: 0;
  overflow-x: hidden;
  overflow-y: auto;
}
section.au-animate {
  padding: 20px;
  position: absolute;
  width: 100%;
  height: 100%;
}
.page1 {
  background-color: lightskyblue;
}
```

```
.page2 {
  background-color: limegreen;
}
/* Slide Animation */
section.au-enter-active {
  animation: slideInRight 1s;
}
section.au-leave-active {
  animation: slideOutLeft 1s;
}
@keyframes slideInRight {
  0% { transform: translate3d(100%, 0, 0); }
  100% { transform: none; }
}
@keyframes slideOutLeft {
  0% { transform: none; }
  100% { transform: translate3d(-100%, 0, 0); }
}
/* Fade In Animation */
.list-animation {
  padding: 20px;
  list-style: none;
}
li.au-enter {
  opacity: 0 !important;
}
li.au-enter-active {
  animation: fadeIn 1s;
}
li.au-leave-active {
  animation: fadeOut 1s;
}
@keyframes fadeIn {
  0%   { opacity: 0; }
  100% { opacity: 1; }
```

```
}
@keyframes fadeOut {
  0%   { opacity: 1; }
  100% { opacity: 0; }
}
```

The upper part of the CSS hasn't changed. What we are interested in is the part from the comment "Fade In Animation" and below. You can see that we provide some initial styling to our UL element that had the "list-animation" class. We then have 'au-enter' definition that sets the opacity to zero (0). When the 'au-enter-active' class is added to our LI, then we call our fadeIn animation with a duration of one second. Likewise, when an item is removed from the list, the 'au-leave-active' class is added and we call the fadeout animation with a duration of one second as well. Both the fadeIn and fadeOut animations set the opacity from zero (0) to one (1) or the inverse correspondingly.

Figure 21-2 shows page3 with our list after we added one donut.

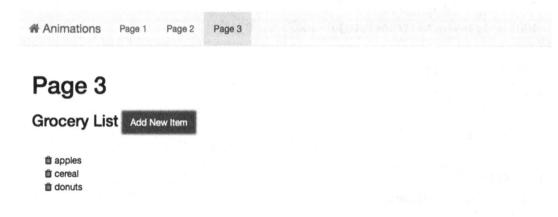

Figure 21-2. *List animation*

Click the Add New Item button or the trash icon to add or remove items from the list. You will see an animation for each that takes one (1) second to complete. Play with the CSS to adjust the settings. Change the CSS to affect other aspects of the element's style. This is just the tip of the iceberg as far as what you can do in your own applications. Don't be afraid to experiment.

Summary

Animations are cool and can take your application from good to great! Be careful not to put animations on everything but wisely choose the places where it makes sense and provides that added user experience benefit. In this chapter we took a look at using the aurelia-animator-css plug-in. We played with using it for our router during navigation as well as with adding and removing items from a list. There are many more scenarios that you can use animations for, but this provides the foundation of where to start. We also identified other plug-ins that work in Aurelia to provide animations. Take some time to look at them as well and select the one that best fits your application requirements. You should now be armed with the ability to provide smooth animations for your own applications.

CHAPTER 22

Dialogs

One common scenario that you will find while building your applications is prompting users for information. You will build views that will represent data entry, but there will be times when you will want to display a dialog. The aurelia-dialog plug-in is perfect for this scenario. In this chapter, we will cover installing and using the aurelia-dialog. We will walk you through using the plug-in and discuss the various workflows you might want to support in your applications. Let's start by installing the plug-in.

Aurelia Dialog Plug-in

In order to use the aurelia-dialog plug-in in your application, you will need to install it. You can do this by executing the following command in your terminal window:

```
au install aurelia-dialog
```

This should automatically put an entry in your aurelia.json file under the aurelia_ project folder. The entry should look like the following under the dependencies section:

```
{
  "name": "aurelia-dialog.js",
  "dependencies": [
    {
      "name": "aurelia-dialog",
      "main": "aurelia-dialog",
      "path": "../node_modules/aurelia-dialog/dist/amd",
      "resources": []
    }
  ]
}
```

© Matthew Duffield 2018
M. Duffield, *Practical App Development with Aurelia*, https://doi.org/10.1007/978-1-4842-3402-0_22

Next, you need to update your main.js file to include the plug-in as seen in the following:

```
import environment from './environment';

export function configure(aurelia) {
  aurelia.use
    .standardConfiguration()
    .feature('resources')
    .plugin('aurelia-dialog');

  if (environment.debug) {
    aurelia.use.developmentLogging();
  }

  if (environment.testing) {
    aurelia.use.plugin('aurelia-testing');
  }

  aurelia.start().then(() => aurelia.setRoot());
}
```

As you can see from the preceding, we are simply bringing in the aurelia-dialog plug-in using the plug-in function from the aurelia.use object.

Now that we have the plug-in installed, let's focus on creating our first dialog. We will create a confirm delete dialog. Consider the following prompt.html file:

```
<template>
  <ux-dialog>
    <ux-dialog-header>${model.header}</ux-dialog-header>
    <ux-dialog-body>
      ${model.prompt}
    </ux-dialog-body>
    <ux-dialog-footer>
      <button click.trigger="controller.cancel()">Cancel</button>
      <button click.trigger="controller.ok(true)">OK</button>
    </ux-dialog-footer>
  </ux-dialog>
</template>
```

The aurelia-dialog comes with several custom elements that are used:

- ux-dialog – this is the root custom element that hosts the rest of the child elements

- ux-dialog-header – this represents the header information

- ux-dialog-body – this represents the body information

- ux-dialog-footer – this represents the footer information

In the preceding example, you can see that we are expecting a model object where we are binding to a 'header' property and a 'prompt' property in the body. We also reference the controller to call either 'cancel()' or 'ok(true)' functions in the footer. Clicking either the cancel or OK button will close the dialog and invoke the 'whenClosed' promise callback. We will look at how this works shortly.

Let's now look at the prompt.js file:

```
import {DialogController} from 'aurelia-dialog';

export class Prompt {
  static inject = [DialogController];

  model = {};

  constructor(controller) {
    this.controller = controller;
  }
  activate(model){
    this.model = model;
  }
}
```

This is a pretty simple view model. We import and inject an instance of a DialogController from the aurelia-dialog plug-in. It is this controller that we use for providing user interaction on the dialog. We also are implementing the activate function passing in a model. It is through this model that we are binding the 'header' and 'prompt' properties in the dialog. Let's now look at what it takes to make use of our newly created prompt dialog. Consider the following app.html file:

```
<template>
  <require from="./app.css"></require>
  <section>
    <h1>${message}</h1>
    <button class="btn btn-primary"
      click.delegate="submit()">Submit</button>
  </section>
</template>
```

In the preceding markup, we are going to display the dialog when the user clicks the submit button. Here is a screenshot of what the app.html view would look like (Figure 22-1).

Launch Dialog

Submit

Figure 22-1. *App.html*

Let's now look at the app.js file and see how we get our dialog to be displayed:

```
import {DialogService} from 'aurelia-dialog';
import {Prompt} from './prompt';
import 'jQuery';
import 'bootstrap';

export class App {
  static inject = [DialogService];

  message = "Launch Dialog";

  constructor(dialogService) {
    this.dialogService = dialogService;
  }
```

```
submit(){
  let model = {
    header: "Confirm Delete",
    prompt: `Are you sure you want to delete this record?`
  };
  this.dialogService.open({
    view model: Prompt, model: model, lock: false
  }).whenClosed(response => {
    if (!response.wasCancelled) {
      console.log('perform delete');
    } else {
      console.log('delete cancelled');
    }
  });
}
}
```

We start off by importing the DialogService from the aurelia-dialog plug-in. It is this service which allows us to interact with our dialogs. Next, we import our prompt dialog that we just created. In the submit function, we configure a model object to be passed to the 'open' function of the DialogService. In the model, we are passing both header and prompt text. Next, we call 'open' on the DialogService passing an object literal. The object literal has three properties:

- view model – this represents the view model of the dialog to be displayed

- model – this represents the model the dialog will use for binding

- lock – this represents whether the dialog will act like a modal dialog or not

The 'open' function is a promise and fires a 'whenClosed' function when the dialog closes. It provides a single response object that will contain a 'wasCancelled' property, so you can determine if the user closed the dialog by cancelling or closed the dialog by clicking the OK button, for example.

Let's take a look at how our dialog looks when we click the submit button from the app.html view (Figure 22-2).

Launch Dialog

Figure 22-2. *Prompt dialog open*

If we open the Debugger Tools and look at the console, we will see two different logs depending on how we close the dialog. Let's first look at what we see when we click the OK button (Figure 22-3).

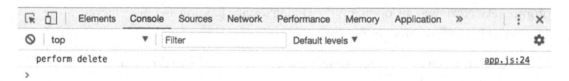

Figure 22-3. *Prompt dialog OK button*

If we launch the dialog again and this time click the cancel button, you will see the result shown in Figure 22-4.

Figure 22-4. *Prompt dialog cancel button*

Although this is a simple example of a dialog, you can incorporate as much business logic around using dialogs as you like. You can even use dialogs to display if a view is dirty and the user is trying to navigate away without saving.

Global Dialog Settings

It is possible to provide global settings concerning how you use dialogs in your application. This helps reduce some of the configuration settings you would need to pass to the 'open' function. You would provide these types settings in the main.js file:

```
export function configure(aurelia) {
  aurelia.use
    .standardConfiguration()
    .developmentLogging()
    .plugin('aurelia-dialog', config => {
      config.useDefaults();
      config.settings.lock = true;
      config.settings.centerHorizontalOnly = false;
      config.settings.startingZIndex = 5;
      config.settings.keyboard = true;
    });

  aurelia.start().then(a => a.setRoot());
}
```

Here you can see that we are providing several settings with the plug-in. We are setting the lock property to true. This means that all dialogs will be treated as modals, unless overridden. Most of these properties are self-explanatory. Remember that you can override any of these global settings by simply providing them in the object literal that is provided in the 'open' function.

Styling Dialogs

It is possible to customize the style of the dialogs that are rendered with simple CSS. Consider the following CSS snippet:

```
ux-dialog-overlay.active {
  background-color: #000;
  opacity: .5;
}
```

By providing this CSS, Figure 22-5 appears.

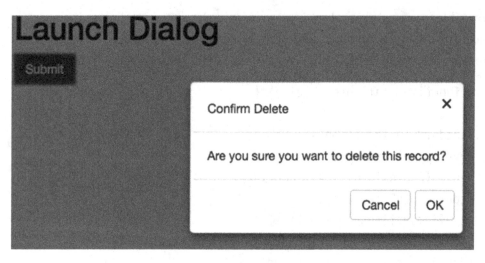

Figure 22-5. *Prompt dialog with custom style*

This gives you the ability to have custom dialog styles to meet your application styles with very little effort.

Summary

In this chapter, we were exposed to using the aurelia-dialog plug-in. We learned how to install the plug-in as well as how to get it set up for use in our applications. We built a custom dialog and looked at what it took to display a dialog. We also learned how to provide global settings for dialogs in our application to help keep our code free from unnecessary ceremony. We finally looked at how we can style our dialogs so that they would look and feel just like the rest of our application. Take some time to play with the aurelia-dialog plug-in. There are other features and lower-level APIs that you can tap into if you need. Above all, have fun playing with the plug-in and get your applications supporting dialogs today.

CHAPTER 23

Localization

You have your application completed and business is booming. However, your boss just walked in and said to you that the application now needs to support Spanish and other languages soon. This requirement could be daunting just by itself but Aurelia has an excellent plug-in that will make supporting multiple languages fairly easy. In this chapter we are going to take a look at aurelia-i18n and how to install and configure it for use in your application. We will look at the conventions required to get your translations hosted on the server and then test your application in both English and Spanish. Let's get started.

Aurelia i18n Plug-in

In order to use the aurelia-i18n plug-in in your application, you will need to install it. You can do this by executing the following command in your terminal window:

```
au install aurelia-i18n
```

This should automatically put an entry in your aurelia.json file under the aurelia_ project folder. The entry should look like the following under the dependencies section:

```
{
  "name": "aurelia-i18n.js",
  "dependencies": [
    {
      "name": "aurelia-i18n",
      "main": "aurelia-i18n",
      "path": "../node_modules/aurelia-i18n/dist/amd",
      "resources": []
    }
  ]
}
```

© Matthew Duffield 2018
M. Duffield, *Practical App Development with Aurelia*, https://doi.org/10.1007/978-1-4842-3402-0_23

You will also need to install i18next by executing the following command:

```
au install i18next
```

Make sure that the entry in aurelia.json looks like the following:

```
{
  "name": "i18next",
  "main": "i18next",
  "path": "../node_modules/i18next/dist/umd",
  "resources": []
}
```

This is one place where the Aurelia CLI may not get the entry correct.

Let's install our final dependency, i18next-xhr-backend. You can do so by executing the following command:

```
au install i18next-xhr-backend
```

Make sure that the entry in aurelia.json looks like the following:

```
{
  "name": "i18next-xhr-backend",
  "main": "i18nextXHRBackend",
  "path": "../node_modules/i18next-xhr-backend/dist/umd",
  "resources": []
}
```

Again, it is possible that the Aurelia CLI does not get this entry correct.

Next, you need to update your main.js file to include the plug-in as seen in the following:

```
import {I18N, TCustomAttribute} from 'aurelia-i18n';
import XHR from 'i18next-xhr-backend';

export function configure(aurelia) {
  aurelia.use
    .standardConfiguration()
    .developmentLogging()
    .plugin('aurelia-i18n', (instance) => {
      let aliases = ['t', 'i18n'];
```

```
    // add aliases for 't' attribute
    TCustomAttribute.configureAliases(aliases);
    // register backend plugin
    instance.i18next.use(XHR);
    // adapt options to your needs (see http://i18next.com/docs/options/)
    instance.setup({
      backend: {
        loadPath: './locales/{{lng}}/{{ns}}.json'
      },
      lng : 'en',
      attributes : aliases,
      fallbackLng : 'en',
      debug : false
    });
  });

  aurelia.start().then(a => a.setRoot());
}
```

We start off by importing I18N, TCustomAttribute, and XHR from the respective
resources. Next, we provide some configuration logic to get localization set up properly.
We are electing to use the i18next-xhr-backend as the loader for the translations. In
the setup, we define where our locale translations are stored. We also identify what our
default language is as well as the attributes that will be available in our markup. We
provide a fallback language and whether or not we want debug enabled. Notice that we
are using the TCustomAttribute to help with configuring the 't' and 'i18n' attributes. This
is necessary to make sure the aliases are defined before rendering the templates.

Let's now look at how we use this plug-in in our app.js file:

```
import {I18N} from 'aurelia-i18n';

export class App {
  static inject = [I18N];

  constructor(i18n) {
    this.i18n = i18n;
    this.i18n
      .setLocale('en-US')
```

```
      .then(() => {
        console.log('Locale is ready!');
      });
  }
}
```

As you can see from the preceding, we import the I18N object and simply set the locale to 'en-US'. Let's see what our app.html file looks like:

```
<template>
  <require from="./app.css"></require>
  <section>
    <h3 t="title">Title</h3>
    <p>
      Translation with Variables: <br />
      ${ 'score' | t: {'score': 13}}
    </p>
    <p>
      Translation singular: <br />
      ${ 'lives' | t: { 'count': 1 } }
    </p>
    <p>
      Translation plural: <br />
      ${ 'lives' | t: { 'count': 2 } }
    </p>
    <p>
      Translation without/with context: <br />
      ${ 'friend' | t } <br />
      ${ 'friend' | t: { context: 'male' } } <br />
      ${ 'friend' | t: { context: 'female' } }
    </p>
  </section>
</template>
```

As you can see from the preceding, we are using the value converter 't' in our string interpolation that uses the string as the key and also has an object literal that provides more meta information for the translation. We also have an example of using the custom attribute 't' that contains the key to be used. Take note that whatever we put inside our markup like we have in the H3 element will be replaced with the translation. You can also use the 'i18n' custom attribute to perform the same.

Figure 23-1 renders our English translation.

Translations in Aurelia

Translation with Variables:
Score: 13

Translation singular:
1 life remaining

Translation plural:
2 lives remaining

Translation without/with context:
A friend
A boyfriend
A girlfriend

Figure 23-1. *i18n using English*

Let's look at what the translation.json file looks like for English:

```
{
  "score": "Score: {{score}}",
  "lives": "{{count}} life remaining",
  "lives_plural": "{{count}} lives remaining",
  "friend": "A friend",
  "friend_male": "A boyfriend",
  "friend_female": "A girlfriend"
}
```

If you are unfamiliar with the syntax, take some time and review the documentation provided by i18n. If we want to try another language, we simply need to create the corresponding folder and provide a translation.json file. Here is a Spanish version that resides under the 'es' folder:

```
{
  "score": "Puntos: {{score}}",
  "lives": "{{count}} vida disponible",
  "lives_plural": "{{count}} vidas disponibles",
  "friend": "Un amigo",
  "friend_male": "Un novio",
  "friend_female": "Una novia"
}
```

It becomes fairly easy to ensure that your application supports localization. Figure 23-2 shows the result when we change the locale to 'es' in our app.js file.

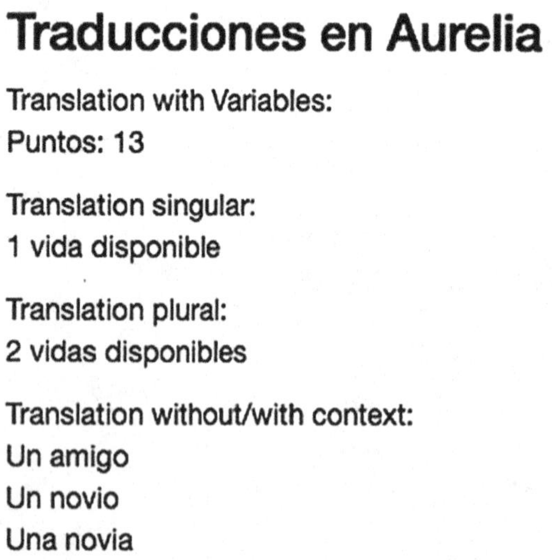

Traducciones en Aurelia

Translation with Variables:
Puntos: 13

Translation singular:
1 vida disponible

Translation plural:
2 vidas disponibles

Translation without/with context:
Un amigo
Un novio
Una novia

Figure 23-2. *i18n using Spanish*

Translations with nested objects

It is possible to use translation objects that have nested properties. Consider the following translation.json file:

```
{
  "header": {
    "title": "Welcome"
  },
  "title": "Translations in Aurelia",
  "score": "Score: {{score}}",
  "lives": "{{count}} life remaining",
  "lives_plural": "{{count}} lives remaining",
  "friend": "A friend",
  "friend_male": "A boyfriend",
  "friend_female": "A girlfriend"
}
```

You can easily access the title property off of the header. Here is an example of the app.html accessing it:

```
<template>
  <require from="./app.css"></require>
  <section>
    <h3 t="title">Title</h3>
    <h3 i18n="header.title">Title</h3>
    <p>
      Translation with Variables: <br />
      ${ 'score' | t: {'score': 13}}
    </p>
    <p>
      Translation singular: <br />
      ${ 'lives' | t: { 'count': 1 } }
    </p>
    <p>
      Translation plural: <br />
      ${ 'lives' | t: { 'count': 2 } }
    </p>
```

```
  <p>
    Translation without/with context: <br />
    ${ 'friend' | t } <br />
    ${ 'friend' | t: { context: 'male' } } <br />
    ${ 'friend' | t: { context: 'female' } }
  </p>
 </section>
</template>
```

Notice that we are using the 'i18n' custom attribute. We are also simply supplying 'header.title' as the value of the attribute for it to perform its translation. You can also do this using the 't' custom attribute.

Summary

In this chapter, we took a look at how we could get our applications to support localization with very little overhead. We were able to configure our application to make use of translations as well as created translation folders on the server to be served for a given locale. This library opens up the door to getting your application truly global. Take some time playing with the plug-in as well as looking at i18n to learn about all of the capabilities available to you. Hopefully, you now have a good appreciation for what aurelia-i18n brings to the table.

CHAPTER 24

Testing and Debugging

We all like to think that we build bug-free applications, but sometimes the unthinkable happens and you find a bug. Building applications with Aurelia is no different, and having a solid testing workflow will help ensure that you deliver solid quality applications. In this chapter we will look at writing tests as well as some tips for debugging your applications in the browser.

Unit Testing

We have been focusing on building applications using the Aurelia CLI. If you created a project and chose not to do unit testing, now might be a good time to create a new project and ensure that unit tests are included in your project. This will simply give you a head start and have the system configured for performing your tests.

Once you have a working project that supports unit testing, you can easily launch your tests by executing the following command in the terminal:

```
au test
```

If you want to have a more test-driven workflow, you can continue to write code and tests without ever leaving your favorite editor by executing the following command in the terminal:

```
au test --watch
```

If you want to write tests for an existing project, you can still install the aurelia-testing plug-in by executing the following command in the terminal:

```
au install aurelia-testing
```

Now that we have everything configured, let's write our first test!

© Matthew Duffield 2018
M. Duffield, *Practical App Development with Aurelia*, https://doi.org/10.1007/978-1-4842-3402-0_24

Testing Custom Elements

Let's write a test for a simple name-tag custom element. The following is the name-tag.html file:

```
<template>
  <require from="./name-tag.css"></require>
  <div class="header">
    <h3>HELLO</h3>
    <h4>my name is</h4>
  </div>
  <div class="body">
    ${name}
  </div>
  <div class="footer"></div>
</template>
```

Here is the name-tag.js file:

```
import {customElement, bindable} from 'aurelia-framework';


@customElement('name-tag')
export class NameTag {
  @bindable name = "Aurelia";
}
```

For completeness, here is the name-tag.css file:

```
name-tag {
  display: inline-block;
  color: white;
  background: #ED2B88;
  border-radius: 6px;
  min-width: 325px;
  text-align: center;
  box-shadow: 0 0 5px rgba(0,0,0,.5);
}
```

```css
name-tag > .header {
  margin: 16px 0;
}
name-tag > .header > h3 {
  font-weight: bold;
  font-family: 'Source Sans Pro';
  letter-spacing: 4px;
  font-size: 32px;
}
name-tag > .header > h4 {
  margin-top: 0;
  font-family: sans-serif;
  font-size: 18px;
}
name-tag > .body {
  background: white;
  color: black;
  padding: 32px 8px;
  font-size: 42px;
  font-family: cursive;
}
name-tag > .footer {
  height: 16px;
}
```

Here is the app.html file using the name-tag custom element:

```html
<template>
  <require from="./app.css"></require>
  <require from="./name-tag"></require>

  <section>
    <name-tag name="Matt"></name-tag>
  </section>
</template>
```

As you can see, we passed in "Matt" to override the default value of "Aurelia". Figure 24-1 shows the result.

Figure 24-1. *name-tag custom element*

Now that we have a custom element created, let's focus on creating our first unit test. Consider the following name-tag.spec file:

```
import {StageComponent} from 'aurelia-testing';
import {bootstrap} from 'aurelia-bootstrapper';

describe('NameTag', () => {
  let component;

  beforeEach(() => {
    component = StageComponent
      .withResources('name-tag')
      .inView('<name-tag name="Matt"></name-tag>')
      .boundTo({ firstName: 'Matt' });
  });

  it('should render name', done => {
    component.create(bootstrap).then(() => {
      const nameElement = document.querySelector('.name-tag-body');
      expect(nameElement.innerHTML).toBe('Matt');
      done();
    }).catch(e => { console.log(e.toString()) });
  });
```

```
afterEach(() => {
  component.dispose();
});
});
```

We are using Jasmine for this example, but Aurelia supports most of the popular testing frameworks. Our test begins with us importing a helper StageComponent object as well as a bootstrap object for getting Aurelia configured.

Next, we are describing the test we are writing, 'NameTag'. You can call it whatever makes sense to you. The describe function takes a callback as its second argument. Inside the callback, you will see that we have beforeEach and afterEach functions. These are used to scaffold our testing scenario.

The it function is what performs the actual test. You can see that we are trying to ensure that we render a name. Remember that the custom element has a default name value, so this should be a good test to ensure that we are overriding the name with the one passed into the custom element. After the component has been created, we check to ensure that the nameElement contains the value 'Matt'.

By following this pattern, you should be able to write tests for all of your components in your application. Custom attributes can be treated exactly the same, with one exception: you will need to be able to reference the element to which the attribute was attached. You can do this by accessing the element property off of the component object in your test.

Mocking Dependencies

It is important that you only focus on testing the component at hand. With that said, you still have to deal with dependencies that are injected into your components. This can be easily handled by mocking your dependencies. Let's consider that the name-tag custom element had a dependency on a NameService which returns a name. The name-tag custom element then binds on a name property exposed on the service. Consider the following test:

```
export class MockService {
    name;

    getName() { return Promise.resolve(this.name);
    }
```

```
describe('NameTag', () => {
  let component;
  let service = new MockService();

  beforeEach(() => {
    service.name = undefined;

    component = StageComponent
      .withResources('name-tag')
      .inView('<name-tag></name-tag>');

    component.bootstrap(aurelia => {
      aurelia.use.standardConfiguration();

      aurelia.container.registerInstance(NameService, service);
    });
  });

  it('should render name', done => {
    service.firstName = 'Matt';

    component.create(bootstrap).then(() => {
      const nameElement = document.querySelector('.name-tag-body');
      expect(nameElement.innerHTML).toBe('Matt');

      done();
    });
  });

  afterEach(() => {
    component.dispose();
  });
});
```

As you can see, it is pretty easy to mock service and dependencies and replace them via the container object.

StageComponent

The StageComponent is a powerful object that provides several helpful properties and functions for us to use during our tests. The following is a list of what is available to you:

- element – refers to the HTML element that is rendered

- view model – refers to the view model of the component

- configure – allows you override the default configuration as well as get a reference to the container instance

- dispose – cleans up the DOM after a test has completed

- bind – allows you to manually handle bind

- unbind – allows you to manually handle unbind

- attached – allows you to manually handle attached

- detached – allows you to manually handle detached

- waitForElement – waits until one element is present or absent

- waitForElements – waits until several elements are present or absent

Feel free to go to the Aurelia documentation and read up on these properties. You will find that you will be able to pretty much support all of your testing needs for your application.

End-to-End Testing

Just as much unit testing is important to ensure that you deliver quality applications, end-to-end testing can provide the peace of mind that your application still works as it should when you are ready to publish a new release. Aurelia uses Protractor for its end-to-end testing tool. Protractor is a mature testing framework that allows you to test your application using the browser. Protractor is beyond the scope of this book, but there is plenty of documentation covering end-to-end testing. Let's see a quick example of what an end-to-end test looks like:

```
describe('aurelia homepage', () => {
  it('should load page', () => {
    browser.get('http://www.aurelia.io');
    expect(browser.getTitle()).toEqual('Home | Aurelia');
  });
});
```

In the preceding example, we see that we are writing a test to ensure that the Aurelia home page loads and gets the title from the browser equaling 'Home | Aurelia'.

Interacting with the Browser

You can also write tests that allow you interact with the browser by sending clicks or typing into forms on the page. The following is an example of navigating to 'http://www.google.com' and then entering the search term 'Aurelia' and clicking the search button.

```
describe('google homepage', () => {
  beforeEach(() => {
    browser.get('http://www.google.com');
  });

  it('should load page', () => {
      element(by.name('q')).sendKeys('Aurelia');
      element(by.name('btnG')).click();

      browser.sleep(2000);
      expect(element(by.css('h3 a')).getText()).toContain('Aurelia');
  });
});
```

Again, it is pretty straightforward to interact with the browser. There are a ton of functions and capabilities that come with Protractor. Take some time to play with it to get comfortable.

This is one area where end-to-end testing is getting easier and easier. Most of the mature end-to-end solutions relay on Selenium as the server to allow for testing, but we are seeing that browser vendors are exposing automation APIs directly. This will really make end-to-end testing easier and less complex but it will be some time before all vendors agree on a common API so that you don't have to fall back on a framework like Protractor and Selenium.

Debugging Aurelia Applications

We all have had to open the developer tools in the browser of choice from time to time to debug our applications. Aurelia comes packaged with two custom attribute helpers that can really make debugging your applications easier:

- view-spy – provides a copy of the view object in the console

- compile-spy – provides the compiler's TargetInstruction

Both of these custom attributes live in the 'aurelia-testing' plug-in, so be sure that you have them installed. Also, you will need to ensure that you have the plug-in loaded in the main.js file:

```
import environment from 'environment';

export function configure(aurelia) {
  aurelia.use
    .standardConfiguration()
    .feature('resources');

  if (environment.debug) {
    aurelia.use.developmentLogging();
  }
  if (environment.testing) {
    aurelia.use.plugin('aurelia-testing');
  }

  aurelia.start().then(() => aurelia.setRoot());
}
```

This ensures that you have access to the 'aurelia-testing' plug-in when you are testing your code.

View-Spy

Let's now look at what it takes to get view-spy working in the app.html file from our previous application:

```
<template>
  <require from="./app.css"></require>
  <require from="./name-tag"></require>
```

```
<section view-spy>
  <name-tag name="Matt"></name-tag>
</section>
</template>
```

As you can see from the preceding, it is simply a matter of adding the 'view-spy' custom attribute to the element you wish. Figure 24-2 shows what it looks like in the browser.

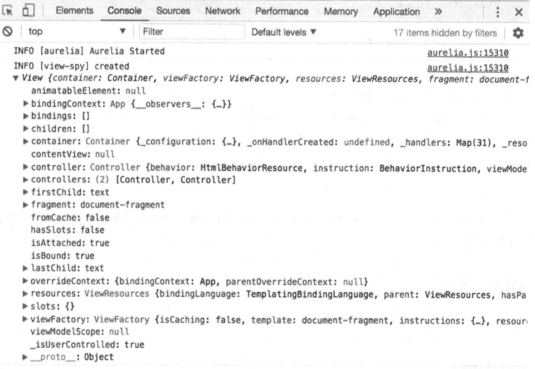

Figure 24-2. view-spy

This one custom attribute provides a wealth of information as you debug your application.

Compile-Spy

Now, let's take a look at what compile-spy brings to the table. Consider the same app. html file again:

```
<template>
  <require from="./app.css"></require>
  <require from="./name-tag"></require>

  <section compile-spy>
    <name-tag name="Matt"></name-tag>
  </section>
</template>
```

As you can see from the preceding, it is simply a matter of adding the 'compile-spy' custom attribute to the element you wish. Figure 24-3 shows what it looks like in the browser.

Figure 24-3. *compile-spy*

We see now that we are exposed to the TargetInstruction. Again, this gives us a lot of visibility into our application.

Aurelia Inspector in Chrome

The final debugging tool that will make your development process easy is the Aurelia Inspector. This is a Chrome plug-in that adds a new inspector pane to the Elements panel, providing information concerning Aurelia for a given selected element. You can install it by searching for it in the Chrome Web Store. Figure 24-4 shows the tool after searching.

Figure 24-4. *Aurelia Inspector for Chrome*

Once you have the inspector installed, you can find it in the Elements pane. The rest simply depends on which element you select. Figure 24-5 is a screenshot selecting the name-tag custom element.

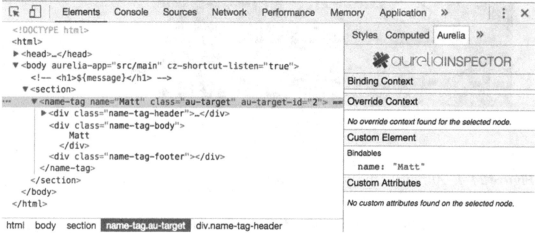

Figure 24-5. *Aurelia Inspector in action*

By now, you should feel pretty confident that you have an excellent set of tools for your debugging experience. Take some time to play with each to get a handle on what information you can gather about your application.

Summary

In this chapter, we took a high-level look at both unit and end-to-end testing. We also looked at several tools to help you with debugging your applications. Writing bug-free applications is a challenge, but with these tools at your disposal, you should feel a little better that you will have fewer bugs in your application.

CHAPTER 25

Bundling and Deploying

At some point during your development workflow, you will want to test your application bundled either on your local dev machine or remotely on a server. The Aurelia CLI makes this very easy to do. In this chapter we will walk you through the steps it takes to bundle your application as well as to create a custom bundle. Next, we will discuss options for deploying your application to a GitHub or Bitbucket account for quick and easy testing.

Bundling

The Aurelia CLI already bundles your application regardless of what environment you are targeting. The following are the steps to bundle your application for debugging:

```
au build
```

This is all that you need to do in order to generate a bundle for development environment. Also, whenever you are running your application or using the watch flag, the Aurelia CLI is generating a bundle for you behind the scenes.

© Matthew Duffield 2018
M. Duffield, *Practical App Development with Aurelia*, https://doi.org/10.1007/978-1-4842-3402-0_25

Figure 25-1 is a sample output of building your bundle.

```
● ● ●                    📁 aurelia-bundle — -bash — 80×45
[starfighter:aurelia-bundle matt$ au build                                      ]
Starting 'readProjectConfiguration'...
Finished 'readProjectConfiguration'
Starting 'processMarkup'...
Starting 'processCSS'...
Starting 'copyFiles'...
Starting 'configureEnvironment'...
Finished 'copyFiles'
Finished 'processCSS'
Finished 'processMarkup'
Finished 'configureEnvironment'
Starting 'buildJavaScript'...
Finished 'buildJavaScript'
Starting 'writeBundles'...
Tracing app...
Tracing environment...
Tracing main...
Tracing resources/index...
Tracing app...
Tracing aurelia-binding...
Tracing aurelia-bootstrapper...
Tracing aurelia-dependency-injection...
Tracing aurelia-event-aggregator...
Tracing aurelia-framework...
Tracing aurelia-history...
Tracing aurelia-history-browser...
Tracing aurelia-loader-default...
Tracing aurelia-logging-console...
Tracing aurelia-pal-browser...
Tracing aurelia-route-recognizer...
Tracing aurelia-router...
Tracing aurelia-templating-binding...
Tracing aurelia-templating-resources...
Tracing aurelia-templating-router...
Tracing aurelia-testing...
Tracing text...
Writing app-bundle.js...
Writing vendor-bundle.js...
Finished 'writeBundles'
starfighter:aurelia-bundle matt$ ▉
```

Figure 25-1. *au build*

The Aurelia CLI will produce the bundle and put it in the scripts folder. Figure 25-2 shows what this folder looks like after the build.

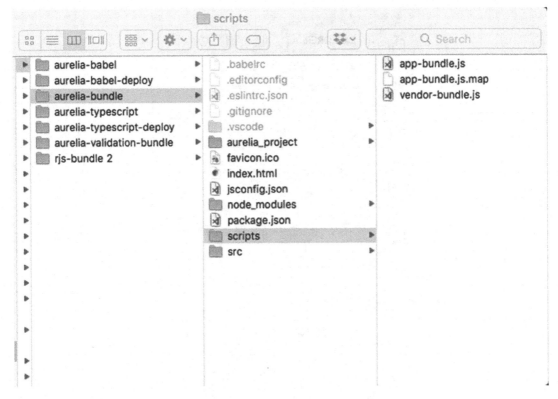

Figure 25-2. *Build output*

As you can see from the figure, the build process created three files:

- app-bundle.js

- app-bundle.js.map

- vendor-bundle.js

We can also target specific environments for our build process. Let's now create a build for production:

```
au build --env prod
```

We use the --env flag to indicate which environment we want to target. This will generate the same files with the exception of the app-bundle.js.map file.

It is also possible to further configure how the Aurelia CLI performs the build. If you look under the aurelia_project folder, you will see three folders: environments, generators, and tasks. Figure 25-3 shows the folders expanded.

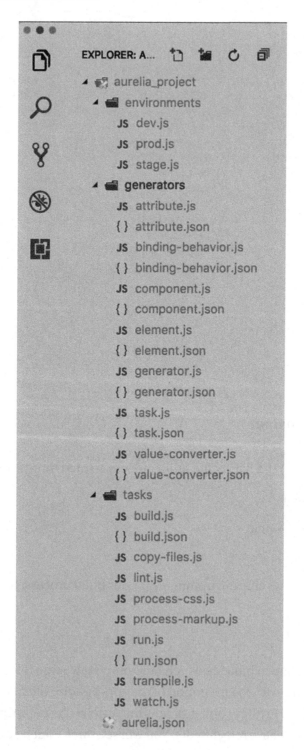

Figure 25-3. *aurelia_project*

The environments folder gives you the ability to define variables that can be used during runtime so that your application behaves differently based on the target environment. For example, opening the dev.js file will display the contents shown in Figure 25-4.

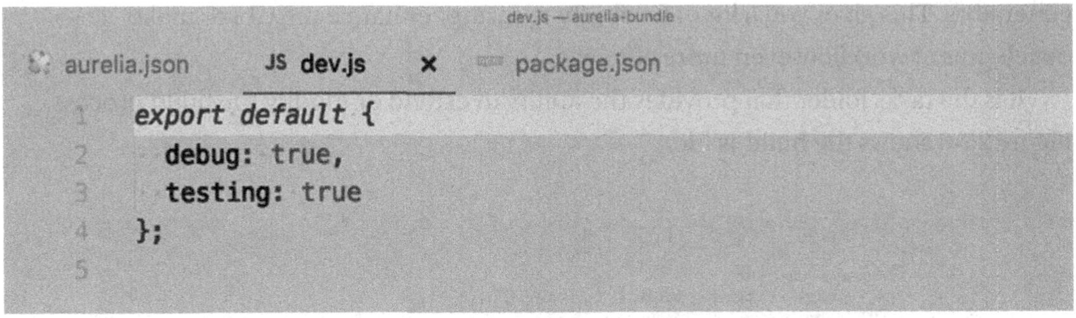

Figure 25-4. *Environment variables for the dev environment*

For each environment, you can change the following variables: debug and testing. A perfect example of how this is used can be seen in the main.js file (Figure 25-5).

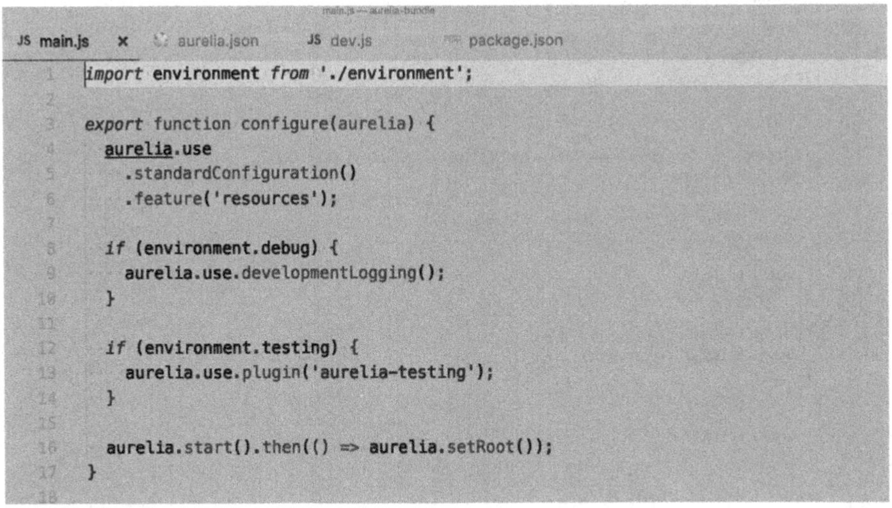

Figure 25-5. *Using environment variables*

You could easily add more variables to each environment file and then use the similar technique shown in the main.js file to use it during runtime. Just make sure that you update all of the environment files so that the build process brings the correct settings.

The generators folder is how you can extend the Aurelia CLI to add custom generators. This gives you a lot of flexibility to further enhance the CLI to make development workflow even more efficient.

It is the tasks folder that provides the ability to extend or modify the build process. Figure 25-6 shows the build.js file.

```js
import gulp from 'gulp';
import {CLIOptions, build as buildCLI} from 'aurelia-cli';
import transpile from './transpile';
import processMarkup from './process-markup';
import processCSS from './process-css';
import copyFiles from './copy-files';
import watch from './watch';
import project from '../aurelia.json';

let build = gulp.series(
  readProjectConfiguration,
  gulp.parallel(
    transpile,
    processMarkup,
    processCSS,
    copyFiles
  ),
  writeBundles
);

let main;

if (CLIOptions.taskName() === 'build' && CLIOptions.hasFlag('watch')) {
  main = gulp.series(
    build,
    (done) => { watch(); done(); }
  );
} else {
  main = build;
}

function readProjectConfiguration() {
  return buildCLI.src(project);
}

function writeBundles() {
  return buildCLI.dest();
}

export { main as default };
```

Figure 25-6. *Aurelia build.js*

As you can see, the Aurelia CLI simply is using GulpJS as its workhorse to perform its operations. It is pretty easy to create a custom task and then inject the task as either a parallel or synchronous task in the build process.

Figure 25-7 shows aurelia.json.

```json
{
  "name": "aurelia-validation-bundle",
  "type": "project:application",
  "bundler": {
    "id": "cli",
    "displayName": "Aurelia-CLI"
  },
  "build": {
    "targets": [
      {
        "id": "web",
        "displayName": "Web",
        "index": "index.html",
        "baseDir": ".",
        "output": "scripts"
      }
    ],
    "options": {
      "minify": "stage & prod",
      "sourcemaps": "dev & stage"
    },
    "bundles": [
      {
        "name": "app-bundle.js",
        "source": [
          "[**/*.js]",
          "**/*.{css,html}"
        ]
      },
      {
        "name": "vendor-bundle.js",
        "prepend": [
          "node_modules/bluebird/js/browser/bluebird.core.js",
          {
            "path": "node_modules/aurelia-cli/lib/resources/scripts/configure-bluebird-no-long-
            "env": "stage & prod"
          },
          {
            "path": "node_modules/aurelia-cli/lib/resources/scripts/configure-bluebird.js",
            "env": "dev"
          },
```

Figure 25-7. *aurelia.json*

261

This file is what drives the Aurelia CLI. All configurations and settings begin here and then are further defined in the corresponding behaviorial aspects of the CLI. In the preceding example, you can see that we have two bundles showing: app-bundle.js and vendor-bundle.js. We can introduce other bundles as well. Consider the following JSON snippet:

```
{
  "name": "aurelia-dialog",
  "main": "aurelia-dialog",
  "path": "../node_modules/aurelia-dialog/dist/amd",
  "resources": []
}
```

This will create the file aurelia-dialog.js in the scripts folder. This gives us the ability to create specific bundles of our application or dependencies instead of bundling everything into a single file. You may want to create a public and private bundle that contains application code that corresponds to whether or not the user is authenticated. You may not want to load the whole application bundle if the user never authenticates or visits screens that require authentication.

The Aurelia CLI is a powerful tool that provides a lot of flexibility and customization for your build and bundling process.

Let's now look at what it takes to deploy our application.

Deploying

After you have built your application for the environment of choice, you are ready to deploy. In order to deploy your application, you only need to ship the following files and folders:

- index.html

- scripts/

You can easily ship the scripts folder and the index.html file to any web server you wish and have it work without any other configuration. If you would like your application to be part of your source control workflow, whether continuous integration or continuous delivery, you can use GitHub or Bitbucket and have your application published once you commit the pages aspect of each. Granted, this won't be exactly the same workflow as you would take when publishing to production, but it gives you a nice feeling to know that your application is working not only on your development machine.

The following steps will guide you through setting up a GitHub or Bitbucket repository for hosting your application. It is recommended that you maintain the publish repository separate from your development repository. This will allow the publish repository to contain only the bundled files necessary to run the application. The development repository will be your full application along with any development dependencies. These steps assume that you already have a development repository set up in place.

1. Create a user account on GitHub or Bitbucket

2. Create a deployment repository. Give it a meaningful name that implies that this repository will be used for deployment

3. Clone this newly created repository onto your local development machine

4. From your separate development repository, execute the following command:

   ```
   au build --env prod
   ```

5. Next, copy the index.html file and the scripts folder from your current development project into the newly created repository

6. Using your Git tool of choice or a terminal window, add these files to your repository

7. Commit your changes to the new repository

8. Push your changes

9. Test your application by navigating to either of the following:

   a. For Bitbucket: `http://<user account>.bitbucket.io`

   b. For GitHub: `http://<user account>.github.io`

These steps come in handy if you are simply wanting to ensure that your application works on machines besides your development machine. It is also a nice complement to your source control workflow.

Note   It may be necessary to go to the settings of repository and turn on pages so that it will host your application.

Deployment Best Practices

Although the Aurelia CLI tries to handle most of the common conventions for you, it is important to be aware of best practices when deploying.

- Use a bundler to minimize and obfuscate (uglify) your code. The Aurelia CLI already does then when you build against the 'prod' environment

- Consider using server-side rendering to help with search engine optimization and client-side optimization. Aurelia supports server-side render. Refer to the documentation for more information

- Never store third-party keys or passwords in your source code

- Consider configuring your hosting server to use HTTPS

- Take care not to use generic wildcards when configuring and setting up CORS

- Consider enabling the 'rev' option for the production build to provide suffix build numbers to help with browser caching once you deploy your application

Summary

In this chapter, we looked at the build process and what the Aurelia CLI provides out of the box. We looked at what it took to bundle our application as well as to create a custom bundle. Finally, we looked at what files and folders are required to deploy our application and reviewed some best practices. You should feel pretty confident with your understanding of the Aurelia CLI regarding builds and have a good feel for deploying.

CHAPTER 26

Closing Thoughts

Building web applications is no small feat. It is possible to build these applications without a front-end framework but it will take considerably more time and headache to do so. Don't be worried about being a newbie when it comes to using Aurelia. The community is great and the Gitter channel and Discourse web site is extremely helpful as you proceed with your development.

As you build your applications using Aurelia, here are a few tips and tricks to help you mitigate spending hours over a certain issue or bug in your code:

- Don't be afraid to ask questions on the Gitter channel, Discourse web site, or StackOverflow. You will be surprised that other developers have the same question.

- Use convention over configuration. Aurelia really shines in this area and once you understand the conventions things will become second nature to you.

- Don't be afraid to use the Aurelia Inspector for Chrome. It will become a huge help as you are testing and debugging your application.

- Don't forget about view-spy and compile-spy. These will also help you when you are scratching your head trying to understand what is happening.

- Iterate often and test even more often. This will help you find just one bug at a time and not a batch at a time as you develop. The CLI helps makes this easy with the live reload feature using (—watch) to keep your browser up to date.

© Matthew Duffield 2018
M. Duffield, *Practical App Development with Aurelia*, https://doi.org/10.1007/978-1-4842-3402-0_26

- Start small and progressively build your application up. If you don't need a specific plug-in don't even bring it in until you need it. This will help keep your application smaller during the bundling phase and will remove unnecessary resources.

- Prefix your custom elements, attributes, value-converters, and behaviors with a unique value. This will help mitigate against third-party plug-ins using the same names.

- Don't simply use two-way data binding when building your pages. If you know that the element never needs to update after the first time, use one-time instead.

- Try to make yourself familiar with Aurelia's view and component life cycle. This will really help you to know when things happen on a page.

- If you get stuck with a problem, sometimes it just helps to step away from your computer and take a walk or find something else to do for a while and then return back to the problem. This can really help you resolve the problem without getting frustrated and allows your brain to work on the problem in the background.

Index

A

Advanced custom element
  bindable properties, 142
  class-level variables, 141
  development toolset, 139
  DIV element, 140
  EventAggregator, 141
  page3.html, 144
  page3.js ViewModel, 145
  selectedTab property, 142
  SLOT element, 140
  SPAN element, 141
  tab-control, 139–140, 143, 145
  tab-item.html file, 142
Animation plug-ins, 211
Aurelia
  convention over
    configuration, 1
  ECMAScript
    specifications, 1
  framework, 1
  routing, 2
  standards-based, 1
  tips and tricks, 265–266
  TypeScript, 1
  uses, 3
Aurelia-animator-css plug-in
  adding/removing items, 217
  app.css file, 215
  app.html file, 213

'au-enter-active' and 'au-leave-active'
  animations, 216
  CSS3 animations, 212
  install, 213
  list animation, 222
  main.js file, 213
  router definition, app.js file, 215
  router-view custom
    element, 212
  slide animation, 217
  viewmodel, page1.js, 214
Aurelia CLI, 3, 262
  build options, 7
  code editor, 14
  CSS processor, 13
  dependencies, 8
  ECMAScript 2015, 9
  generation, 20
  Hello World, 21–22
  help, 18–19
  installation, 8
  install dependencies, 16
  new project, 11
  NodeJS, 9
  project review, 15
  template minification, 12
  transpiler selection, 12
  unit testing, 13
Aurelia-fetch-client, 56
Aurelia-http-client plug-in, 69, 71

© Matthew Duffield 2018
M. Duffield, *Practical App Development with Aurelia*, https://doi.org/10.1007/978-1-4842-3402-0

B

Binding behaviors, 97
    BindingSignaler initial load, 173
    debounce, 171
    oneTime, 174
    self, 174
    signal, 172
    throttle, 171
    updateTrigger, 172
BindingBehaviorView, 176
Bundling
    app-bundle.js and
        vendor-bundle.js, 262
    app-bundle.js.map file, 257
    application for debugging, 255
    au build, 256
    aurelia.json, 261
    aurelia_project, 258
    build.js file, 260
    build process, 257
    dev environment, 259
    environment variables, 259
    JSON snippet, 262

C

Child routers, 33–35
Child view ports, 35–37
Circle custom attribute, 156
Compile-spy, 251–252
Component life cycles
    flexibility, power, 119
    hooks
        attached(), 119
        bind(bindingContext,
          overrideContext), 118
        constructor, 118
        created(owningView, myView), 118
        detached(), 119
        unbind(), 119
Compose
    app.js file, 181
    app.js view-model, 181
    custom elements, 179
    customer screen, 180–183
Conditional expressions, 102
Container management, 57–58
Controller, 112
CSS3 animations, 212
Custom attributes
    circle, 156
    definition, 147
    input-mask, 150
    set-focus, 147–150
Custom binding
        behaviors, 174–176
Custom elements
    addToOptions function, 134
    advanced custom elements (*see*
        Advanced custom element)
    aurelia-framework, 133
    child custom element, 130
    definition, 127
    properties, 133
    removeFromOptions, 134
    select function, 134
    standard custom elements (*see*
        Standard custom elements)
    static custom elements (*see* Static
        custom elements)

D

Data binding
    behaviors, 97
    binding scopes, 95

check box, 83–85

class/style, 91–93

conditionals, 93–94

element content, 90

input element, 83

looping, 96

radio buttons, 86–87

referencing elements, 82

select control, 87, 89

types, 81

value converters, 97

Datalist, 131

DataService, 47

DateFormat value converter, 164

Debugging aurelia applications

    aurelia inspector in
        chrome, 252–254

    compile-spy, 251–252

    plug-in, main.js file, 249

    view-Spy, 249–250

Dependency injection (DI)

    autoinjection, 55

    container management, 57–58

    containers, 56–57

    decorator, 54

    definition, 51

    manual injection, 52–53

    resolvers, 58

    tried-and-true approach, 51

Deploying

    best practices, 264

    development repository, 263

    files and folders, 262

    GitHub/Bitbucket repository, 263

Dialogs

    aurelia-dialog plug-in

        App.html, 227, 228

        custom elements, 227

        DialogController, 227

        DialogService, 229

        installation, 225

        main.js file, 226

        object literal properties, 229

        prompt dialog open, 230

        prompt.html file, 226

        prompt.js file, 227

    global settings, 231

    styling, 231

DOM events

    bindings types, 98

    call, 99

    delegate, 98–99

    trigger, 99

Dynamic routes, 30–32

Dynamic views

    enhance

        page3.html file, 190–191

        rendered view, 189

        'submit' function, 192

        'update' function, 192

        viewTemplate
          property, 190, 192

    getViewStrategy

        InlineViewStrategy, 187

        page1.js, 185–186

        page2.js, 186

        rendering view, 189

E

End-to-end testing, 247–248

ES6 and TypeScript, 9

Event aggregation

    data binding approach, 126

    shell setup (*see* Shell setup)

    subscriptions management, 125–126

F

Fallback route, 41–42
Features, 195–196
Front-end framework, need of
    requirements, 3
        single-page application, 3
        solving complex patterns, 3

G

Getting data
    HTTP Client
        API functions, 71–72
        aurelia-http-client
          plug-in, 69, 71
        'content' property, 69
        fluent API approach, 72
        functions, 73–74
        helper function, 69
        HttpResponseMessage and
          properties, 72
        retrieving data, 70
        'styles.css' file, 70–71
        view-model, 68
    HTTP Fetch Client, 74–76
getViewStrategy function, 185
GithubService, 64
Global dialog settings, 231
Global resources configuration, 196–197

H

HTML form element
    aurelia.json, 109
    aurelia.use object, 110
    BootstrapFormRenderer
        implementation, 112
        render function, 114
    controller, 112
    invalid email registration-form, 115
    invalid registration-form, 114
    plug-in inclusion, 110
    registration-form, 110–112
    simple form, 107–109
    single class property, 108
    'submit()', 108
    user interface, 108
    'validate', binding behavior, 111
    ValidationControllerFactory, 112
    ValidationRules object, 112
    valid registration-form, 115
    view model, 108
HTTP Client interceptor, 76–79
HTTP Fetch Client, 74–76

I, J, K, L

i18n plug-in
    app.html file, 236
    app.js file, 235
    dependencies, 233
    i18next-xhr-backend, 234, 235
    installation, 234
    main.js file, updation, 234
    TCustomAttribute, 235
    translation
        English, 237
        nested objects, 239–240
        Spanish, 238
InlineViewStrategy, 185
Input-mask custom attribute, 150

M

Markup Scenario, 198–199
Mocking dependencies, 245
Model-view-view-model (MVVM), 2

N, O

'nav-bar' custom element, 23
NodeJS, 9–10

P, Q

Plug-ins creation
    Aurelia CLI project, 208
    bundles array, 202
    custom attribute, 210
    file structure, 201
    input-mask.js bundle, 203
    installed plug-in, 209–210
    publish, 208–209
Push state configuration, 29

R

Routing
    child routers, 33–35
    configuration
        CSS markup, 28
        markup elements, 27
        nav-bar.html file, 26–27
        properties, RouteConfig
            object, 25
        RouteConfig
            objects, 24–25
        'router-view' custom
            element, 23
    configureRouter, 24
    dynamic routes, 30–32
    fallback, 41–42
    layouts, 37–39
    push state configuration, 29
    redirecting routes, 40
    unknown routes, 40–41
    view ports, 35–37

S

Security and pipelines
    audit step
        back-end service, 47
        DataService, 47
        pipeline setup, 48
        web API back end, 47
    authorize step, 44
        addAuthorizeStep, 45
        property, 45
        run function, 46
        SecurityService class, 46
    router pipelines
        pipeline addition, 44
        router classes, 43
        slot lists, 43
Services
    app.css file, 64–66
    app.html file, 63
    app.js file, 62
    dependency injection, 62
    GithubService, 64
    github-service.js, 61–62
Set-focus custom
        attribute, 147–150
Shell setup
    'active-view' message, 124–125
    app.html file, 122–123
    app.js file, 123–124
    class level property, 125
    customers view, 122
    EventAggregator, 124
    home.html file, 124
    'payload', 124
    products view, 122
    router-view changes, 122
    "title", 124
    'viewTitle', 124

Sort value converter, 167

Standard custom elements

    datalist, 131

    multi-selector.css, 135–137

    multiselector custom element, 129, 139

    multi-selector.html file, 130

    multi-selector-item.html

        ViewModel, 134–135

    page2.html use, 137–138

    removeOne function, 135

    Twitter Bootstrap, 138

    ViewModel, 131–133

Static custom elements

    creation

        app.html file, custom

          element use, 129

        bindable attribute, 129

        HTML requirements, 128

        nav-bar custom element, 129

        router property, 129

        template tag, 129

    navigation menu implementation, 127

    static markup bound, 127

StopPropagationBindingBehavior, 174

String interpolation, 101–102

T

Templates

    "as-element" attribute, 105–106

    composition, 105

    conditional expressions, 102

    slots, 104

    static, 101

    string interpolation, 101–102

    view resource pipeline, 103

Testing

    end-to-end testing, 247–248

    unit testing (*see* Unit testing)

TimeAgo value converter, 162

U

Unit testing

    command

        au install aurelia-testing, 241

        au test, 241

    custom elements, 242

    mocking dependencies, 245

V, W, X, Y, Z

Value converters

    class, 162

    conventions, 161

    databind value converter

        parameters, 163

    DateFormat, 164

    functions, 161

    globalResources function, 169–170

    "modifiedDateTime" property, 162

    multiple parameters, 163–167

    parameters as objects, 168–169

    sort, 167

    TimeAgo, 162

    view-model values, 161

View life cycles 117–118

View-Spy, 249–250

Get the eBook for only $5!

Why limit yourself?

With most of our titles available in both PDF and ePUB format, you can access your content wherever and however you wish—on your PC, phone, tablet, or reader.

Since you've purchased this print book, we are happy to offer you the eBook for just $5.

To learn more, go to http://www.apress.com/companion or contact support@apress.com.

Apress®

Printed in the United States
By Bookmasters